D1145242

THE MANUAL OF MODERN PHOTOGRAPHY

KISSELBACH AND WINDISCH

THE MANUAL
OF
MODERN PHOTOGRAPHY

English Translation:
F. Bradley, A. I. B. P., A. R. P. S.

Third edition
Fully revised

HEERING-VERLAG
SEEBRUCK AM CHIEMSEE
1971

Title of the Original German Edition:
NEUE FOTO-SCHULE

Printed in Germany
© 1971 by Heering-Verlag GmbH, Seebruck am Chiemsee, West Germany.
Only authorised English translation.
All rights including that of reproduction in whole or in part expressly reserved.
Printed by Wilh. Friedr. Mayr, Buchdruckerei, Miesbach / Obb.
ISBN 3 7763 1320 X

CONTENTS

"Even books have their Hour of Fate — and become bestsellers. This is not the reward of ambition; it is a gift, good fortune, some would even call it an act of grace."

Let us cast our minds back to the Thirties. 9 × 12 cm was the conventional camera format, 6 × 9 was already looked at askance. Those who worked with smaller formats still were considered beyond the pale. All the standard text books of photography and formularies were hidebound.

The Leica and the Rollei put an end to this changeless tradition. The log-jam was broken. Evolution? No — revolution! New ideas could no longer be stifled, "Die Neue Foto-Schule" (German title of this book) no longer be ignored. We devoured it, to us it was a new Bible. Thirty years ago it was hot from the press, exciting, fascinating, unique — and has remained so ever since.

That it became an instant bestseller it owed to its Hour of Fate; that it held its ground for more than a quarter of a century to its solid substance, to Windisch, the man who interpreted this substance to his readers.

The author of the world's most successful guide book of photography, Hans Windisch, is no longer among us. Is this a reason why we should forget his work and name, which for decades was a household word most intimately bound up with the success of the 35 mm format?

Only what is continually brought up to date has a chance to survive.

We cannot thank the publisher enough for having persuaded Theo Kisselbach to undertake the task of reviving this work. There is no need to introduce Kisselbach, his reputation as a thorough writer on the subject of 35 mm photography augurs well for the success of this great project. A true master has been called upon to save a great man of photography from undeserved oblivion; he wrote this book in honour of and gratitude to Hans Windisch; his readers, present and future, will benefit from it as their fathers did thirty years ago.

Prof. Stefan Kruckenhauser

This book deals with "photography today". It shows you the way as simply and clearly as possible. Hans Windisch's style was ebullient. Without much ado he went straight to the heart of the matter. This method has been retained. Photography has become simpler within the last thirty years, but only from the technical aspect. If you expect results that are useful, you cannot succeed without a little mental effort. You must know why you take your photograph, what the picture is intended to convey. You will find that photography has its uses in every walk of life, not only as a hobby and for taking visual notes on your holiday trips. It can help you to record important situations and events in almost all professional fields.

Photography should come as easily and simply to the user as writing a letter. Some schools already teach photography as a subject; unfortunately they are few and far between, although it is important to become familiar with it as early in life as possible.

This "Manual of Modern Photography" is intended to assist you in taking better photographs. An early tradition had it that the way to proficiency led through the photographer's own darkroom. This still holds good today, even if the conditions have changed. We now no longer waste our time making up developers according to various formulae. We use ready-bought kits for both the negative and the positive processes. The technical side of photography is merely auxiliary. The picture is the decisive factor.

You will produce good pictures only if you learn how to see properly; this is why this book begins with the chapter "The eye for a picture". The visual medium today makes a far stronger impact on us than in days gone by. Even the daily papers have almost become illustrated papers. And television has left the steam radio far behind in popularity.

This book hopes to teach mainly by visual precept and example, according to the principle that a picture says more than a thousand words. Don't say "I am not technically minded" — say "I am inexperienced". Practise as often as you can, and you will be surprised how soon you will be able to handle your camera with complete assurance. You must be able to use it subconsciously as it were, so that you can concentrate your attention on the picture. It is like driving a car: while you still have to think when you are using your clutch and changing your gears you will be a bad driver. The much quicker reaction occurs without mental control if your reaction is automatically correct. This, too, you will achieve only by regular and frequent practice.

If you take pictures only once a year, you will always remain a beginner. And if you travel after such a long interval, more's the pity if you are not quick enough to catch the most interesting situations.

You will find many recommendations and warnings in this book. But all these tips are useful only if you try them out in actual practice. You may safely forget all the technical advice if following it has become second nature to you through the frequent use of your camera.

On many occasions trial films are recommended; almost invariably black-and-white films will be satisfactory here. They are merely processed and evaluated as negatives. Don't moan about the cost. It is the cheapest method of acquiring an efficient technique. Nor should you ask about how many frills a photographic outfit has; the question should be "what is of real use to me, if I can handle it perfectly?"

Find out how smoothly you can release your shutter, how quickly you can focus, whether all the controls are convenient to operate. Mostly this is more important than enthusiastic sales talk that does not help you when you are in difficulties.

If you are a beginner do not expect to be a good photographer as soon as you have finished reading this book. The manual part of photography calls for a certain amount of dexterity that can be acquired only through practice. Your mind must remain free for pictorial considerations and such simple questions as "What" "When" "Where" "How" "Why" "What for" "For whom" "What with".

When your mental processes and technique are smoothly coordinated you will soon reach the stage that I have used as a yardstick for the conception of this book. And I am sure you will agree with me: photography is much too important in everyday life to be treated as a weekend hobby.

THE EYE FOR A PICTURE

The great mass of enthusiastic amateurs taking pictures on the most varied occasions — of their families or on holidays — relive their experiences through the medium of photography. It is, the best aide memoire we know, because our normal capacity for remembering things is so very limited and inaccurate. There is a variety of possibilities that enable us to photograph a subject in such a way that the picture becomes more than a mere likeness.

Pictures are the most important information medium of our age. The illustrated press, the trade journals, the daily papers need photographs. Scientists and technologists record the results of their research by means of photographic evidence. It is both an aid to and a record of their work. Indeed, sometimes only a photograph will enable us to recognize an event or a fact, because without the aid of the camera our eye would be unable to perceive it.

The realism of a good photograph is unequalled by any other method of representation. Photography therefore has the reputation of being honest and above board as a recording medium. But the results obtained with the camera can be very varied, and the nature of representation is by no means as self-evident as it would appear at first sight.

In addition to all the familiar uses the field of pure recording has become an increasingly important application of photography, because of the ability of this medium to store innumerable visual symbols within a tiny fraction of a second. Some of these operations are controlled by fully automatic apparatus. Some instruments, on the other hand, require their users to master the basic principles of photography in order to obtain the best possible results without fail.

Photographic physics and chemistry are complicated, but their practical application has become so simplified that nobody should find it difficult. Better viewfinders help us to select our subjects with more confidence, higher lens speeds combined with ultra-fast emulsions allow us to take photographs even in poor lighting conditions, and we can find the correct exposure either by means of automatic exposure control or with a very sensitive exposure meter. As with driving a car it is no longer necessary to take an interest in the internal working of the mechanism involved. All we have to know to be able to handle a camera are the simple operations: focusing, setting the lens stop and shutter speed, and releasing the shutter.

The eye and the camera

In spite of all the technological progress made the fundamental task remains of deciding what we want to photograph — the choice of subject, i.e. of what we find valuable, of what will be of use to us, and of the moment when to press the button. All this will continue to be a matter of the photographer's personal decision.

We are surprised that the beginner, even if he is intellectually very agile, will not find on the film what he really had wanted to photograph. Many a textbook compares eye and camera to each other just because some of their functions run parallel. In reality seeing and photographing are not at all the same: although our eye includes a lens and a light-sensitive layer the process of vision proper will enter our consciousness only through its connection with the brain.

Of all our sense organs the eye is the most important to us. Scientific investigations have shown that 73 % of all information reaching us about the most varied events come to us through the eye. For our photographic practice it is therefore useful to know how the eye functions.

Let us first regard the eye as a camera. A diagrammatic cross section shows the outer cover of the choroid, the aqueous humour, the iris with the adaptable pupil, the lens, the vitreous body, and the retina. Light enters the eye, and depending on its intensity the pupil dilates or contracts — i.e. it automatically controls the intensity of the light. The formation of a sharp image on the retina calls for individual focusing, which depends on the distance of the object. Since the lens itself cannot change its distance, its shape and refractive power are changed by means of muscular power.

The illustrations show how this change is brought about. We speak of the accommodation of the eye, i.e. the eye focuses on the object. The presence of a certain minimum quantity of light is essential to this function. The retina consists of light-sensitive cells, the photo-receptors. In the centre are the cones, about 7 millions of them, surrounded by more than 120 m. rods. These are most sensitive, but not to colours; they therefore become active only in poor lighting conditions. The cones, on the other hand, are much less sensitive, but are able to recognize colours. We see with them in good light.

The light-sensitive substance proper is the rhodopsin, also called visual purple. It is chemically changed by the action of light. The nerves pass on the

12

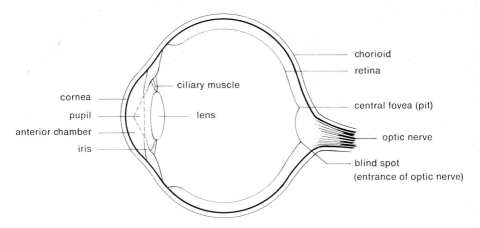

cornea

pupil

anterior chamber

iris

ciliary muscle

lens

chorioid

retina

central fovea (pit)

optic nerve

blind spot
(entrance of optic nerve)

Diagrammatic section through the eye

Normal eye

*Shape of the lens in
distant accommodation.*

*Shape of the lens
in close-up accommo-
dation.*

Longsighted eye

*Eyeball too short
Lens thickened even
for distant objects.*

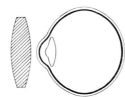

*Additional positive
lens allows close-up
accommodation.*

Shortsighted eye

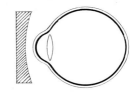

*Eyeball too long
Negative lens
extends the rays,
so that the distance
is in sharp focus.*

*Shortsighted persons
can focus close-up
objects without
optical aid.*

distance

close-up

This representation ignores the fact that with increasing age the eye loses its ability to accommodate itself.

A small transparency frame, which you should always carry on you, is a useful aid to finding the right picture area from the most favourable point of view.

At a distance of 50 mm from the eye the picture area will correspond to that of the standard focal length of the 35 mm format. If we increase the distance the picture area will be changed.

In the bottom picture the distance between the frame and the eye is 90 mm. The picture area inside the frame corresponds to that of a 90 mm camera lens.

The pictures on the facing page of Stuttgart-Echterdingen Airport show how this works in practice. The smaller area of the bottom picture of course occupies the entire frame of the film after exposure.

Photographs on facing page by Hans Steinhorst

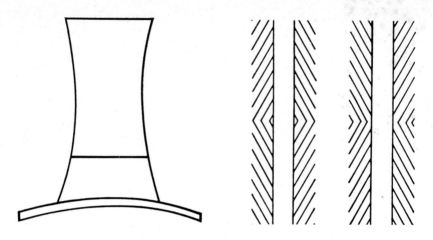

Optical illusions. They readily prove the frequent inaccuracy of our visual perception.

The height of the top hat appears to be greater than the width across the brim. In the drawing on the right the arrangement of the lines simulates divergence and convergence of the parallels. The direction of the arrowheads also influences our eye, and lines of equal length appear to be longer or shorter depending on the direction of the arrowhead.

Movement is suggested by the rhythm of the wavy lines in the drawing by Ridget Riley (below).

relevant impulses electrically to the brain. Since we see consciously only via the brain, this constitutes an important difference between eye and camera.

Many events are correctly perceived only because of this influence of the brain. The position of the image projected on the back of the eye is upside down. However, since in order to behave correctly we need an upright image, this is rotated through 180° by the brain. Likewise the brain makes a correction so that the environment remains stationary when we look around, moving our head. Even when we are travelling in a vehicle, the surroundings appear to be standing still. On the other hand, the impression of movement is accurately registered when objects of the surroundings move.

The visual angle of the eye is considerable both in the horizontal and in the vertical direction. But we see only a very small sector really sharp. We scan, as it were, the objects we are interested in one after the other and store the total information in the brain only if it is of real interest to us. In a photograph, however, all image points are recorded indiscriminately by a single exposure.

The difference between eye and camera described now is of even greater significance. The focal length of our eyelens can be varied within narrow limits to enable us to see both distant and close-up features in sharp focus. Since it would adversely affect our behaviour if we saw objects in our environment at different sizes all the time, a certain adaptation takes place automatically during a change in object distance. A few examples will explain this:

Normally a door is 7 ft high; its reproduction ratio, when the door is seen at a distance first of 23 ft, and then of 11 ft 6 in, by no means changes in exactly the same way as on a photograph taken at both these distances. We are even more strongly aware of this difference when we look at heads of about the same size from a distance of 3 ft 4 in and of 10 ft. The head 3 ft 4 in away is not seen three times as large as the one at 10 ft. This automatic adaptation subconsciously prevents the beginner from utilizing his film frame effectively. He will take a photograph, for instance, of a person by a fountain from 70 ft away without considering that with a camera lens of standard focal length the person will be reproduced at much too small a scale.

The camera follows a very important rule: it forms its images according to the Law of Central Projection. It is significant that in pictorial reproduction the attempt to prove this method of representation mathematically and to introduce it as an aid to perspectively correct rendering in painting was not made until the 15th Century. Leonardo da Vinci used this central projection in a classical manner in his famous painting "The Last Supper" (p. 24). As central projection and realism became commonplace through photography, creative art turned more and more towards subjective and abstract forms.

In every photograph perspective depends on the camera position. The angle of view is changed depending on whether we use a lens of extremely short, medium, long, or ultra-long focal length in our camera. But it does not affect the perspective; the only difference consists in the fact that a given subject area is reproduced smaller or larger.

A simple gadget enables us to perceive this change clearly: when we look through an empty 5 × 5 cm slide frame held in front of one eye at a distance the length of a matchstick, keeping the other eye closed, it will frame the picture area of a standard-focal-length lens. If we hold it closer, we notice the wide-angle effect. Conversely, at a longer distance, the changes evident in longer-focal-length pictures will become prominent.

The view through the frame corresponds to that through the viewfinder. We now see all the reference points, the correct proportions of the lines and areas within the picture. Whereas in binocular vision we recognize the relationship between fore- and background insufficiently, we now have a good control enabling us to avoid disturbing intersections. We can always carry the little frame in our pocket. It is a valuable aid to training our eye to see "like a camera".

The frame also shows us what changes will occur when we use a lens of different focal length. If we increase the distance from the eye to 90 mm, the picture area will correspond to that covered by a 90 mm lens, and if we increase it to 200 mm, to that of a 200 mm lens. Often pictorial composition will become more compact with longer-focal-length lenses; unimportant features will be cut off, important ones become larger and more prominent. Playing about with our little frame will also make us realize how many more photographic possibilities exist all around us if we are not confined to a single focal length. Above all it teaches us to pay attention to one of the most important rules of photography: "Utilize your film format."

Light and colour

To photograph means "to draw with light". Light is a sensory perception triggered by electromagnetic vibrations (waves). The human eye perceives these vibrations only within a wave length range of 400—700 nm. Some animals react to the infra-red waves longer than 700 nm, others to the ultra-violet waves shorter than 400 nm. If certain conditions are met a longer range than that covered by the eye can be used photographically. Within this narrow waveband our receptor, the eye, is sensitive to many wave lengths. It reports not only "light", but also its "stations", the colours.

We perceive direct sunlight with a proportion of light reflected by the blue sky and a few white clouds as white daylight. Light as such is not visible. What we see is only the reflection of objects struck by the light.

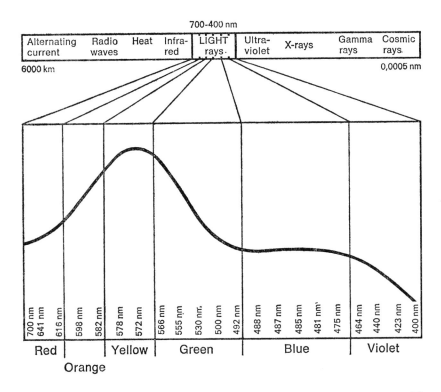

If we pass a "white" light ray through a prism (which differentially refracts the various wave lengths), a "spectrum" appears as if by magic (Lat: spectrum = ghost). What we see are spectral colours, not body colours.

But even the body colours (pigments) show that "white" light represents a mixture of colours. Any body we perceive as coloured (i.e. even luminous aniline dye) absorbs, swallows, the greater part of the white mixed light, reflecting the rest. This rest is "its own" colour. A red church roof, for instance, absorbs all colours except red, it "is" red. Yellow flowers "are" yellow, since they absorb all colours except yellow. Colour is therefore always a product of light. In darkness all objects are completely colourless. Nor can an object exhibit a colour that is not contained in the light incident on it.

Besides daylight, artificial-light sources also play an important part in photography. The spectral composition of daylight differs widely. Our eye hardly notices minor changes. Only when the blue proportion is almost completely absent, e.g. in the light of the setting sun, do we become aware of the colour shift. The spectrum of ordinary halfwatt light differs greatly from that of daylight. In colour photography these changes appear very prominent. Further details will be found in the relevant chapter.

How does the eye see, how the camera?

Let us summarize the important functional differences between the two.

1) The eye sees in colour. The various colours are perceived at different strength according to the intensity of the light. In black-and-white photography the colours are reproduced in grey tones; we can influence the grey values by using suitable filters.

2) The image seen by the eye disappears after about $1/50$ sec, the photographic image can be recorded permanently.

In this picture the black-and-white contrast is the decisive element. The graphic effect was achieved with a deliberately short exposure. "Normal" exposure on the shadow portions of the worker would have caused halation.
Roof construction. Leica M 3, 35 mm Summicron f/16, $1/500$ sec
Photograph by Rudolf Uthoff.

These six examples convey an impression of the wide range of photographic possibilities: Holidays, sightseeing, science, sports, from infinity to close-up there is not a subject the camera does not record in all its detail.

Top: "Down to the Sea". 50 mm Summicron, ¹/₂₅₀ sec. Photograph by Walter Lueden

Acropolis. Orange filter. Photograph by Kisselbach

Andromeda Nebula. 101 cm Schmidt Camera, f/3.5. Photograph by Dr. Vehrenberg

On the Nuerburgring.
560 mm Telyt, f/8,
1/500 sec. Photograph by
Guenter Osterloh.

Coexistence on a drop
of honey. 90 mm Elmarit,
f/22. Photograph by
Harald Doering.

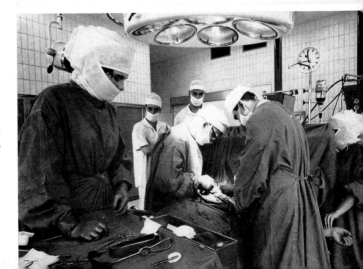

In the operating theatre.
Leicaflex SL,
21 mm Super-Angulon,
f/5.6, 1/60 sec. Photograph
by Guenter Osterloh

Not until the end of the Middle Ages did the painters explore the laws of central projection scientifically. Leonardo da Vinci and Albrecht Duerer took the trouble to record the new knowledge and to publish it.

Duerer's woodcut shows how, with the aid of a dioptre and a frame whose field has been divided into squares by means of wires, only a small section is viewed at a time and transferred to the squared drawing paper.

3) The eye has only a narrow visual angle within which it sees really sharp. It adds up the details in the brain and records only what we are really interested in. The camera indiscriminately records everything situated within its angle of view.

4) The eye has only a limited ability to recognize finest detail beyond a certain distance. Camera lenses of long focal lengths overcome distances.

5) The eye is able to perceive very rapid movement only poorly. Provided the intensity of the light is high enough, photographic exposure material records movements of $1/1000000$ sec duration.

6) The eye requires a certain minimum brightness in order to recognize an object. At a sufficiently long exposure the camera can produce a picture even when the light intensity is below the threshold value necessary for the eye.

7) The eye records only light between 400 and 700 nm. Photographic emulsions record even rays we cannot see.

8) For the eye the minimum distance of comfortable vision is 25 cm. The camera takes many-times magnified close-up- and macrophotographs.

9) We see stereoscopically with both eyes. When we photograph with only one lens, the picture will appear only two-dimensional. Only lighting and perspective create the impression of space.

10) The eye is able to adapt itself to a very wide range of brightnesses of an object; it automatically compensates brightness contrasts. The film in the camera can accommodate great brightness contrast only within limits.

11) The eye adapts itself to different distances so rapidly that we see everything in sharp focus simultaneously. Depending on focusing, aperture, and focal length of the lens, the camera shows a clear difference between sharp and unsharp zones.

12) Eye and brain are integrated. We often see objects not as they are, but as we want to see them. Moreover, we prefer some features to others. The camera lens, on the other hand, reproduces important and unimportant elements with equal emphasis.

13) The eye does not see objects according to their true distance. A camera records exactly according to distance and angle of view.

14) The eye is comparatively insensitive to minor colour shifts. It automatically corrects, for instance, the colour shift caused by halfwatt light. The colour film, on the other hand, records these shifts very clearly.

In order to understand the essential nature of photography we must first examine its basic features. It has two aspects: the creative, artistic one, and the technical, mechanical one. The former involves ideas and imagination, the latter manual dexterity and patience. Although we receive many stimuli that induce creativeness, a certain basis must exist. Those who are completely without talent in this field cannot become "artists", no matter how hard they try. This is not a disaster, but it does militate against a career in professional photography.

The technical aspect of photography, on the other hand, is not difficult to grasp and can easily be learned. But then again it is not as simple as those who think that ownership of a camera is equivalent to "being able to take pictures" assume. This book stresses the technical side of photography, explaining it and demonstrating its various facets.

A photograph is a two-dimensional reproduction of a three-dimensional object. We expect of a good picture that the portion it reproduces is only a selection, a concentrate. If we point our camera simply into our surroundings, all we usually see on the film is a welter of meaningless objects. The reproduction can be influenced in a large number of ways. The aspect of our subject changes with the position of the camera. It can also be influenced by a change in the lighting (front, contre-jour, side light). If we have lenses of various focal lengths at our disposal we can considerably modify the pictorial presentation by varying the distance. Before a photograph is taken exploration of the effect of all these factors with our little transparency frame is very useful indeed. At the beginning we shall take whole series of exposures in order to become really familiar with the changes of reality wrought by the photographic process. After all, rendering in black and white involves quite an appreciable transformation of the coloured scene we see.

Photography is an optical language, a picture language, understood throughout the world without translation. A photograph is regarded as an objective rendering of reality. Everybody knows that nothing has been added to a genuine photograph. But since it represents only a portion without the surroundings, a photograph can give an impression completely different from that of the original situation. How subjective photographs are we can recognize by the fact that a given object can be rendered quite differently by different photographers. Each of them will have his own conception of the subject and use different photographic means for its realization.

The recording accuracy of the photographic lens is unequalled by any other medium. By no other means can we record as accurately the abundance of details found, e.g., on a Gothic cathedral. The same applies to the speed with which we can do this; it enables us to take pictures both of very fast-moving objects, and while we are moving ourselves (e. g. in a train), at $^1/_{1000}$ sec.

We can also record certain phases of a movement sequence. It evidently requires a degree of practice to press the button at exactly the right moment. But it is equally important to know what phase is suitable for photography. We must therefore first familiarize ourselves with the event itself, for we must release the shutter a fraction of a second in advance to allow for the intervening time lag before it can act.

The taking of a photograph is therefore by no means a predetermined process. We must decide ourselves, and must consider three conditions as we do so: the camera position, the picture area, and the lighting.

In order to determine the correct camera position we must find the side which shows up our object at its most characteristic. When a child makes a drawing of a bicycle, he will always draw it from the side. To us this presentation is by no means the only one, but if we take the bicycle from another point of view, we should be clear about its effect and photograph it with this purpose in mind.

The picture area is partly affected by the camera position. The relationship between foreground and background is strictly defined by the picture area, depending on whether we take our subject at eyelevel, from the bird's eye view or the worm's eye view. The importance of concentrating the pictorial contents on essentials has already been mentioned elsewhere. Especially in the beginning we should photograph only a few subjects, and make them fill the whole frame.

A detailed chapter of this book is devoted to the influence of the illumination. The correct assessment of the photographic effect of the light requires some practice and experience. At first our eye is easily deceived.

HOW IS A PICTURE PRODUCED?

The technical side of photography, too, rests on three conditions: light, a camera, and light-sensitive material.

The most important part of the camera is the lens. It forms an image of a portion of our surroundings on the light-sensitive emulsion (film). The camera has three control elements which must be set in response to the exposure conditions: the shutter, which regulates the exposure time, the iris diaphragm, which controls the quantity of light passing through the lens and also influences the depth at which the object is reproduced sharply, and the distance setting, with which sharpness is confined to the pictorially important features. The hallmark of a successful photograph is the best possible balance of all three functions appropriate to the individual camera subject.

Light is active in our camera. We therefore use a substance that changes under the influence of the light. We have found such a substance in the silver bromide compounds. They form tiny crystals, which are mixed with a gelatine solution. Further treatment results in the various properties of this "emulsion" which are necessary for our photographic purposes. The emulsion is coated on strips of transparent cellulose; this is cut into films.

The light-sensitive emulsion is "exposed" in our camera, although this does not yet produce a visible image. All the light has done has been to influence the chemical bond between the silver and the bromine physically. Where much light reaches the emulsion many silver bromide crystals are "activated"; where the quantity of light is small, only partial activation takes place. Below the "threshold value" no changes occur. We therefore require a certain minimum quantity of light in order to produce developable changes.

If we now place the film in a suitable chemical solution, the "developer", the silver bromide *struck by light* will be separated into bromine and metallic silver by it. This makes portions affected by the light black (silver) when we view them against the light; the bromine enters into the developer solution. The unexposed silver bromide must now be removed from the emulsion in the fixing bath. Our photographic "negative" is finished! When we hold the film against the light we shall see that the "tone values", i.e. the grey tones on the developed and fixed film, are the exact reverse of reality; a "negative" has been produced. After fixation the film is rinsed and dried; it is now stable.

To obtain a "correct" positive picture we must reverse the negative. For this purpose we place the film on a sheet of light-sensitive paper, which we now expose. Only little light can pass through the dark portions of the negative, much through the light ones. After exposure, the photographic paper, too, is developed, which produces a picture whose grey gradation is the opposite of that of the negative – i. e. it corresponds to reality. Instead of copying the film "by contact", placing it on photographic paper, we can "project" the small negative on the film on to a larger sheet of bromide paper with the aid of an enlarger; this is called "projection printing" or, more popularly, enlarging.

The positive paper print is the final photograph. Since colour photography has appeared on the scene, it is called a black-and-white photograph. It does in fact translate the colours of reality into black-grey-white steps. It can be compared to a pencil drawing from nature rather than to a painting.

Briefly and simply: the principle of the camera

In this chapter the technical concepts of the camera are explained only in general terms. It therefore does not give instructions how to handle a certain camera. The differences between various types are so great that the special directions by their makers must be consulted. At any rate, the technical details are discussed only to the extent necessary for the understanding of the following chapters. No theorizing for the sake of theory.

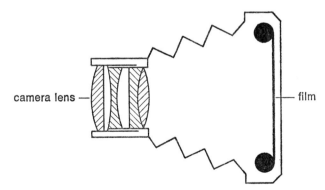

camera lens — | — film

A camera consists of a light-proof housing; the lens is mounted on the front panel, and a device for attaching the light-sensitive film inside the back.

The lens has a decisive influence on photographic reproduction. Every lens, even the most complex one, functions in the final resort as a collecting lens (reading glass). The only difference betweeen the two extremes is in quality, not in kind. A collecting lens combines all the rays arriving from infinity, e.g. from the sun, in a point, called the *focal point*. The distance between the principal point of the lens and the focal point is called the *focal length*.

The opposite of collecting lenses are diverging lenses. They, too, are of importance in lens design. As the drawing shows this lens diverges the incident light rays. Collecting lenses are thicker, diverging lenses thinner in the centre than on the periphery.

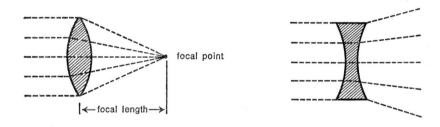

Lenses must not necessarily be of "basic shape" (1 and 4). The following additional shapes are possible:

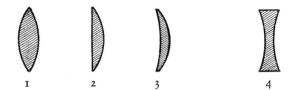

On the left the shapes of the collecting lenses.
1) biconvex, 2) plano-convex,
3) concave-convex.
3) is called a "meniscus" by the opticians. Here it is a +meniscus.

On the right the shapes of the dispersing lenses.
4) biconcave, 5) plano-concave,
6) another meniscus (= "little moon"), this time a —meniscus.

A single lens suffers from a number of aberrations such as curvature of field, spherical aberration, chromatic aberration, astigmatism, coma, and distortion. By means of combining several lenses these aberrations can be reduced sufficiently to have very little, if any, effect on the photographic image. A camera lens consists of several lens elements of various types of glass and precision-calculated radii. Tolerances play an important part in its computation. Slight residual aberrations often affect the *pictorial* reproduction favourably. If we cut off the marginal rays with the iris diaphragm some aberrations disappear completely; others are unaffected by the diaphragm.

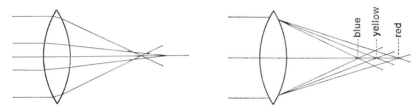

On the left spherical aberration. The marginal rays are more strongly refracted than the central ones.
On the right chromatic aberration. The marginal zone of the lens acts like a prism. The white light is split up into its various colours.

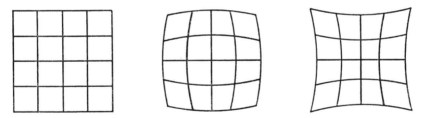

Distortion. Lenses suffering from this fault form either pincushion- or barrel-shaped images of a square, depending on the setting of the diaphragm.

The previously accepted designation of the performance of a lens by the lines per mm it resolves is insufficient for an indication of its quality; too many other factors are involved in the assessment. During the last decade a considerable improvement in lens performance has become evident, because

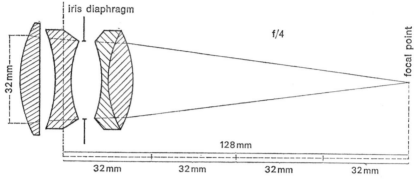

In this example of an f/4 lens, the free aperture of 32 mm is ¹/₄ of the focal length of 128 mm.

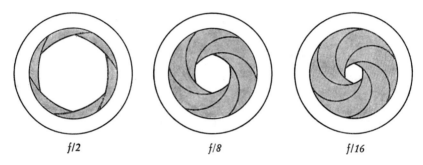

f/2   f/8   f/16

the systems can now be calculated by computers. Whereas 30 years ago the computation of a lens might have taken anything up to a whole year, today it will be complete within a matter of days. But in spite of this progress, lens manufacture still remains a branch of optical precision engineering.

The focal length

The focal length of a lens decides its reproduction scale. A longer focal length produces a larger picture of a given object. It also is the distance at which the lens forms a sharp image of all objects situated at infinity. By infinity we mean a distance that is very long compared with the focal length. The focal length of a lens is engraved on its front mount in cm or mm. In order to obtain a sharp image of nearer objects, we have to increase the distance between the lens and the film plane.

THE SPEED

The speed of a lens is the ratio of its maximum effective diameter to its focal length. We also speak of its "relative aperture" since it is not the actual diameter, but its relation to the focal length that is important to the light transmission. The lens speed is numerically expressed as f/ . . . . where f = free lens diameter. f/2 means that the focal length is twice as long as the free lens diameter.

THE IRIS DIAPHRAGM

An adjustable diaphragm is built into the lens; it serves to reduce its aperture, cuts down its light transmission, and the image formed by the lens on the film becomes correspondingly dimmer. The exposure time must be increased accordingly. The effect of the lens diaphragm resembles that of the iris of our eye; we therefore also call it an iris diaphragm. The engraved aperture values are simplified expressions: only the denominator of the fraction is given. 4 means f/4. The progression of the values has been chosen so that each successive higher number represents half the lens speed (aperture) of its predecessor. The international aperture scale in use today reads as follows:
1   1.4   2   2.8   4   5.6   8   11   16   22   32   45
Since the values are relative, a large number means a small aperture and vice versa.

LIGHT LOSSES IN THE LENS

The theoretical value of the lens speed is somewhat reduced by absorption and reflection inside the lens. Some time ago these losses played an important part, but since the introduction of lens coating (a reflection-reducing film is vapour-deposited on the lens surfaces), they need be considered only with the zoom lenses consisting of 12—15 elements.

ANGLE OF VIEW

The conventional indications refer to the diagonal of the film format. Wide-angle lenses have, as their name implies, a wide angle of view, i.e. they cover a wider area from a given camera position than a standard lens, but at a smaller reproduction scale. With telephoto lenses the angle of view is narrow. In practice, the effect is more striking in the viewfinder or on the focusing screen than the indication in ° would suggest to our imagination.

When a lens is focused on infinity, the distance between it and the film plane (extension) equals its focal length. The extension must be increased beyond the focal length for objects nearer the camera. This longer distance is called image distance. The lens must be focused critically on the correct distance. The closer the object, the more must the extension be increased.

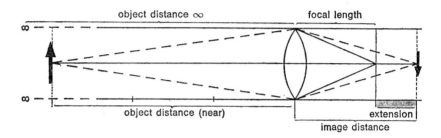

Lens formulae (only for the mathematically minded)

The relationships between focal length, image distance, and object distance are defined by the so-called lens formula:

$$\frac{1}{\text{image distance}} + \frac{1}{\text{object distance}} = \frac{1}{\text{focal length}}$$

Object distance is the distance between the camera lens and the object to be photographed*. The following derivations are possible:

$$\text{Image distance} = \frac{\text{Object distance} \times \text{focal length}}{\text{Object distance} - \text{focal length}}$$

$$\text{Focal length} = \frac{\text{Object distance} \times \text{image distance}}{\text{Object distance} + \text{image distance}}$$

$$\text{Object distance} = \frac{\text{Image distance} \times \text{focal length}}{\text{Image distance} - \text{focal length}}$$

We can calculate also the reproduction scale if image distance and object distance are known, as follows:

---

* On most cameras the distances on the helical mount of the lens refer to film plane — object, not to lens — object.

34

$$\text{Reproduction scale} \quad = \quad \frac{\text{Image distance}}{\text{Object distance}}$$

These formulae are very rarely used in practice. In the near-focusing range, where they are of real significance, we place graph paper in the focusing plane, focus it, and find the reproduction scale very quickly on the basis of the relationship between the mm scale on the original and its dimensions on the groundglass screen.

DEPTH OF FIELD

Whatever is situated in the focusing plane will appear sharp in the image. Whatever is situated in front of it or behind it will appear more or less unsharp. The transition to unsharpness is influenced by the aperture of the iris diaphragm. If this is small, the depth of field will be great. At small apertures, i.e. large numbers, it is therefore possible to form a single sharp image of objects at various distances. Depth of field plays an important part in photography. It is therefore necessary to memorize the examples on p. 39 and to appreciate the effect of and changes in the depth of field by means of taking a series of trial pictures.

Whereas in the past there was often a preference for great depth of field, which led to the use of very small apertures and correspondingly long exposure times, today relatively large apertures are the fashion. The resultant unsharpness of fore- and background is valued as a pictorially creative element. The use of the shorter exposure times this permits offers many practical advantages. The quality of the camera must, however, be very high, so that optimum sharpness is obtained precisely where it is wanted in the picture.

Most lenses have a depth-of-field ring, which shows the aperture numbers to the left and right of the index mark. The extent of the depth of field can be read off against the aperture numbers on the left and right.

Circle of Confusion

Sharpness is a relative concept. What will be adequate for a 13×18 cm (6×8 in) negative would be insufficient for a 35 mm negative, because this small negative must invariably be enlarged, whereas the large format can also be reproduced as a contact print. The concept of sharpness tied to the negative format is defined by the admissible diameter of the circle of confusion. Sharpness is achieved in large formats when the diameter of the circle of confusion does not exceed $1/100$ of the focal length of the lens. A different rule governs the 35 mm negative. The conventional tables and depth-of-field scales on the lenses are calculated for an admissible diameter of the circle of confusion of $1/30$ mm, applying to all focal lengths. This is adequate for ordinary purposes.

For sharpness fanatics

If the demands of sharpness are very strict, this value will be too generous, and it will be better to adopt $1/60$ mm as the admissible diameter of the circle of confusion. Obviously the depth of field is thereby considerably reduced. In practice we can use the conventional tables also for these stringent requirements simply by taking the depth-of-field reading at half the aperture value, i.e. at f/4 when we stop down to f/8.

The shutter

We distinguish between two types: the between-lens shutter and the focal-plane shutter. The former is a blade shutter, which works at optimum efficiency when it is installed between the elements of the camera lens (hence its name). Its blades open and close very rapidly by spring action. Its highest speed is $1/500$ sec. The focal-plane shutter is of advantage in single-lens-reflex and system cameras. Its two roller blinds move directly in front of the film. At high shutter speeds it therefore exposes the film successively. Depending on the width of the slit shutter speeds of up to $1/2000$ sec are possible. Since the closed shutter completely prevents light from reaching the film, lenses and

Top: Setting on ∞, f/4, $1/500$ sec. The foreground is unsharp.
Bottom: At the same lens stop and shutter speed the background is unsharp if the lens is focused on the wrought-iron lantern in the foreground. Nymphenburg Park. In modern photography this "sharp-unsharp" setting is preferred to the earlier technique of radically stopping down for great depth of field.

In the first picture the lens was used at full aperture and focused on the house in the background. Sharpness falls off towards the foreground; the terrier is completely blurred.

Let's try a different method and focus on the man in the middle distance.

In the third picture the lens was focused on the terrier in the foreground; the dog, naturally, appears sharp, with progressive unsharpness towards the middle distance and the background.

Facing page:
A comparison of the pictures shows how the depth of field can be adjusted without a change in the distance setting; merely the lens aperture has been changed. At a large aperture the depth of field is small, at a small aperture great.

accessories can be conveniently changed on the camera. All shutter speeds, even the highest, can be used with all focal lengths and lens speeds.

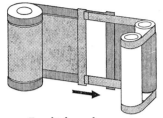

Between-lens shutter   Focal-plane shutter

The speed scale has been arranged so that the next setting always doubles or halves the exposure times. In the engraved scale the numerator of the fraction is omitted: 125 = $1/125$ sec. Here is the scale, or part of it:

2000   1000   500   250   125   60   30   15   8   4   2   1   B*.

When the shutter is set at B it remains open as long as we press the release button.

Whereas in the past shutter speeds were controlled mainly by mechanical means, in future we shall come to rely increasingly on electronic components, which offer, especially with long time exposures, some advantages with automatic exposure control.

Viewfinder cameras

The viewfinder indicates the boundaries of the field. Cameras in the lower price range have a simple viewfinder, the more expensive ones a viewfinder with coupled rangefinder, the most efficient of which is the bright-line viewfinder. One of the bright outlines disappears if we look through the viewfinder obliquely, i.e. wrongly.

The optical design of measuring viewfinder systems with bright-line frames

---

* Where the scale includes the symbol "T", the shutter, at this setting, opens at the first pressure on the release button, but does not close again until the button is pressed a second time.

The same event with two cameras: Top f/4, $1/500$ sec, bottom f/16, $1/30$ sec.
Top: "Frozen" movement, but little depth of field.
Bottom: Movement blur, but great depth of field (see pattern of the carpet).

is considerably more complicated, because here parallax is compensated in the near-focusing range by an ingenious linkage with the distance setting. This compensation is necessary because the viewfinder is mounted a few cm obliquely above the lens.

In the measuring viewfinder the measuring field proper is reflected onto the central viewfinder field. To find the measuring field at the first attempt the following method is recommended: The viewfinder field is blacked out; only the measuring field can now be seen in the viewfinder. When we remove the "black-out", a double image will be visible if the focusing is not accurate. By rotating the helical focusing mount of the lens we can make the two images coincide. The correct distance has now been set.

Twin-lens-reflex cameras

The twin-lens reflex camera has become most popular in the 6×6 cm ($2^1/_4 \times 2^1/_4$ in) format. As the name implies the camera is equipped with two separate lenses, of which the upper serves as viewfinder lens, forming an image of the subject on the groundglass screen via a mirror. The taking lens proper is mounted below the viewfinder lens on a common front panel; both lenses are focused together by means of a fine-adjustment mechanism. The viewfinder lens has no diaphragm; it therefore forms a bright image on the groundglass screen, making focusing very convenient. Here, too, a focusing magnifier as a focusing aid is very useful although it is very weak. The wrong-way-round viewfinder image is slightly disturbing with moving objects.

Single-lens-reflex cameras

35 mm format. In the simple models we observe the image formed by the lens on the focusing screen via a surface mirror. The image is right-way-up, but wrong-way-round. A magnifier is necessary for viewing and accurate focusing. This simple principle can be used only with stationary objects. In the technically more advanced models the viewfinder image is therefore reversed by means of a pentaprism so that right-way-round observation is possible. We are now able to look at the subject directly on the upright format; there is no need to view at an angle of 90 °. This extends what has been the exclusive advantage of the viewfinder camera to the reflex camera.

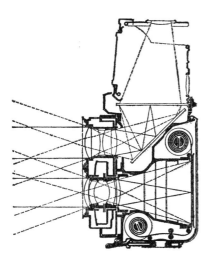

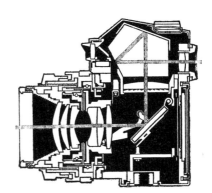

◀ *Twin-lens-reflex camera*

▼ *Single-lens-reflex camera*

6 × 6 cm (2¹/₄ × 2¹/₄ in) format. The 6 × 6 cm (2¹/₄ × 2¹/₄ in) medium format is used in pictorial journalism as well as in general professional work. The negative area is 3.75 × as large as that of the 35 mm format, which has some advantages when colour photographs are to be evaluated for blockmaking. Fewer single-lens-reflex cameras than those of the 35 mm format employ the image-erecting pentaprism, which owing to increased complexity becomes very expensive. The square format, however, makes its use less essential.

FOCUSING SCREENS

All reflex cameras, twin- or single-lens, require a focusing screen. Ground-glass screens exist in many different versions. If their grain is very fine, they will be bright, and we can see all the details very clearly; but there is a risk of "over-focusing", because the image is not clearly enough confined to the focusing plane. Coarse-grained ground-glass screens are not suffering from this drawback, but they are dark, and details are recognizable only with difficulty. Thus the efficiency of a groundglass screen cannot be as much taken for granted as most of us expect.

A number of cameras use a plastic screen in which measuring wedges or a micro-pattern is impressed. These screens are considerably brighter than groundglass screens. The prism wedges or the screen pattern diffuse the light

43

rays when they form an unsharp image. When the object to be reproduced is situated in the focusing plane the double image disappears in the measuring wedge, and flickering ceases in the micro-screen pattern.

With all focusing screens perfect eyesight is essential to photography at full aperture. Slight visual defects are much more frequent than is commonly assumed. These slight defects, which do not call for spectacles and therefore remain uncorrected, create difficulties. Since we use magnifiers for focusing, the visual acuity of the eye for the distance is decisive. An occasional eye test to confirm this would be useful.

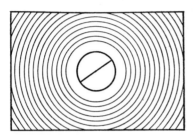 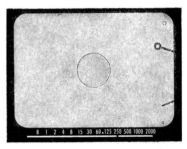

Focusing screens. On the left Fresnel screen with measuring wedge. On the right micro-screen with prism screen in the central circle.

Camera formats

There is no generally valid rule about which camera format is the most favourable. What is decisive is, after all, not the size of the negative, but the quality of the positive, and it is surprising what even the smallest formats can do. Nor need the side ratio of the negative determine the shape of the final print. Unfortunately, only too often is the negative enlarged in its entirety. Square formats have the advantage of the most rational utilization of the lens performance. Nor does the question of vertical versus horizontal camera position arise. Negative areas of any shape and size can be part-enlarged from a square negative without difficulty.

When we assess the usefulness of a format, we must always weigh the advantages against the disadvantages from our personal point of view. Small negatives have the following advantages: light weight, handy shape, and instant readiness for action of the camera: great depth of field at the standard focal

8 × 11 mm = 88 sq. mm

 12 × 17 mm = 204 sq. mm

 18 × 24 mm = 432 sq. mm

 28 × 28 mm = 784 sq. mm

 24 × 36 mm = 864 sq. mm

 4 × 4 cm (38 × 38 mm) = 1444 sq. mm

 6 × 6 cm (56 × 56 mm) = 3136 sq. mm

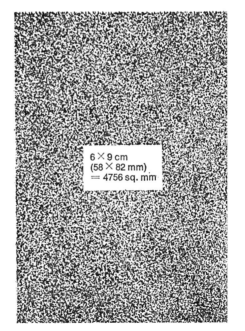 6 × 9 cm (58 × 82 mm) = 4756 sq. mm

length, interchangeable lenses of small bulk and relatively high speed; inexpensive exposure material, any desired quantity of film, high speed of operation, economic processing. The disadvantage is the need for higher enlargement scales, with limits imposed by the resolving power and graininess of the film.

For critical assessment we use enlargements of identical size (about 16 × 24 cm [6 × 10 in]). This means an enlargement of 20 × of the subminiature 8 × 11 mm format, of 6 × of the 35 mm (24 × 36 mm) format, of 4 × of the 6 × 6 cm (2¹/₄ × 2¹/₄ in) (56 × 56 mm) medium format, and of 2 × of the 9 × 12 cm (84 × 110 mm) large format. It is obvious that lower enlarging factors offer advantages at a given standard of technical quality. Here, however, the first practical snags arise: technically flawless negatives are obtained much more quickly with a good 35 mm than with a large-format camera, whose many movements must be mastered by the operator. The majority of users have therefore come down in favour of the 35 mm, and an appreciably smaller number in favour of the medium format. Large-format cameras are preferred for professional purposes.

Subminiature negatives have to be enlarged 8—10 times for the album. Cameras of this format are extremely valuable in the role of a photographic notebook, because they can be our constant companions on account of their light weight. Since the largest ones do not utilize even a quarter of the area of a 35 mm negative they do not approximate the performance of the 35 mm group especially in the field of colour photography. Provided we are aware of these limitations, we shall be able to put these cameras to good and most successful use.

The *28 × 28 mm format* offers many amateurs photography completely without operating problems. Film insertion is made very simple and rapid by the special (Kodapak) cassette. If the camera has a built-in exposure meter, the film speed, too, is automatically set. The 28 × 28 mm format is adequate for all family and holiday subjects. It offers maximum convenience which has ensured it a huge popularity. The price of the film is slightly higher than that of the classical 35 mm film.

The *miniature range* of formats is dominated by the 35 mm (24 × 36 mm) size. With suitable films it is not at all difficult to obtain black-and-white enlargements in the 18 × 24 cm (8 × 10 in) format which satisfy even the most critical eye. The same film is used in 24 × 24 mm and 18 × 24 mm cameras. The number of exposures on a given length of film rises accordingly. Certain limits exist in the field of colour negative films if for professional or scientific reasons maximum resolution is required. No losses of resolution will be noticeable during the projection of colour transparencies.

These limitations become less important with *medium formats* (from 4×4 cm upwards); but to compensate for this, the difficulties of operating the equipment increase. The format ratio of about $1 : 1.5$ of 35 mm to 6×6 cm ($2^1/_4 \times 2^1/_4$ in) requires a 50 % increase in all focal lengths for the larger format. This automatically reduces the depth of field and the range of uses in poor lighting conditions. In good lighting conditions the larger format produces higher resolution, especially in the field of colour photography.

OPERATING THE CAMERA

The format also has a bearing on camera operation. A slightly smaller, lighter camera is handled more conveniently and quickly. Each additional lens and each accessory is lighter or heavier depending on the format for which it has been designed. The decision which format we are going to use is easier if we intend to use only one or two focal lengths.

The method of handling a camera, our release technique with difficult speeds ($^1/_{30}$ and $^1/_{60}$ sec) play a much more important role in actual practice than many theoretical considerations. In order to take good pictures it is essential to be able to carry out all manipulations subconsciously, so that our mind can totally concentrate on the pictorial composition. The illustrations on p. 50 therefore show a comparison of the most varied conditions for a number of important types of camera, with special emphasis on how the camera is held and the shutter released.

An old rule demands that all manipulations shall be carried out in the same sequence for every exposure:

1) Lens stop   2) shutter speed   3) focus   4) shutter release.

With all automatic cameras 1 and 2 have been abolished, which leaves us with 3 and 4. Since we must release the shutter for every exposure, we must pay the most careful attention to this operation.

It is a great handicap if pressing the shutter release in your camera requires some effort. Cameras in which the release is smooth produce sharper pictures. Any force a camera might require for this manipulation can be slightly balanced by the judicious application of counterforce. Any pressure needed on the release button should never have the effect of tilting the camera during the exposure. The procedure should be tested with an empty camera in front of the mirror.

Better still, a test for camera shake should be carried out. About 30 holes are punched in a sheet of dark packing paper (size about 50 × 50 cm) with a 4—5 cm (1 3/4—2 in) nail. The sheet is hung up in front of a window so that we can photograph the holes from a distance of about 1 m (40 in) in bright daylight. Focusing should be as accurate as possible. The shutter speeds should be $1/30$, $1/60$, and $1/125$ sec, and each of them repeated twice or three times. The lens stop depends on the brightness of the light without the sheet of paper. The shape of the holes — crisp and round, or a little blurred — will indicate on the developed negative whether we have a steady hand.

The risk of camera shake increases with the focal length used. Vibrations can occur with telephoto lenses even when the camera is mounted on a tripod. A small glass of water is placed on the camera, the shutter set at $1/30$ sec and released, and the surface of the water observed. Reflex cameras and focal-plane shutters are less steady with long focal lengths than between-lens shutters. If we are photographing stationary objects, we should with very long focal lengths look for a two-point support. Slow shutter speeds (about $1/2$ sec and longer) are often less troublesome than the speeds between $1/8$ and $1/30$ sec.

Some movements appear frozen if we photograph them at very high shutter speeds. During motor cycle and car races the camera must follow the movement of the vehicles. This gives us movement blur in the background which enhances the impression of speed. But in such situations we can also work with slow enough shutter speeds so that the moving object itself becomes blurred. Here the camera must not follow it, because the resulting double movement blur will be found disturbing. With rapid movements we obtain this wipe effect at $1/30$ or $1/60$ sec. Slower shutter speeds require a tripod. The addition of movement blur may produce interesting pictorial effects. If the minimum stop still admits too much light, we can cut this down with a grey filter.

Fountain sculpture, Rome. The slow shutter speed reveals the movement of the water spouts, which lend special attraction to the contours of the figure.
Leica M 3, 200 mm Telyt, f/11, 1/10 sec. Photograph by Siegfried Hartig.

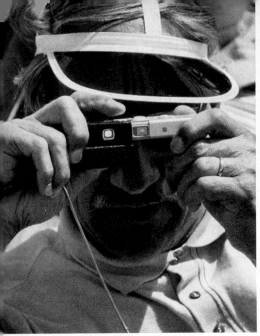

The lighter the camera, the more steadily it must be held because the negatives must be greatly enlarged.

If your vision is equally good on both eyes, use the right eye for looking through the viewfinder; you will be better able to support the camera.

The longer the focal length of the camera lens, the more rigid should the tripod be.

With long-focal-length lenses and still subjects a second tripod for propping up the front part of the lens is a great advantage.

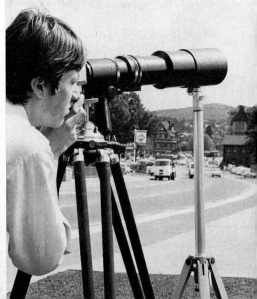

For upright pictures this method of release by the tip of the thumb with counter-pressure by the index finger ensures particularly steady action.

Here the camera is rotated through 180° for another upright view. It is important to prop it against your forehead.

For horizontal pictures, medium-long-focal-length lenses are supported by the angled elbow.

This small table tripod is a very useful gadget on journeys when you have to travel light.

Of all the mishaps owing to wrong handling, blockage of the film transport is the most exasperating. The most careful attention should therefore be paid to the part of the operating instructions dealing with film insertion. Almost all cameras offer checks for correct film transport. In many 35 mm cameras the rewind knob rotates when the film is correctly wound. Only if this check is carried out regularly after each film insertion will our subconscious participate in this check. It is also necessary to follow the correct sequence of the manipulations strictly.

Before we open the back of a camera we must make sure that the film has been rewound. It is equally important to mark the film as exposed and to keep it in a light-tight wrapping. Many pictures at the beginning of a 35 mm film have been spoiled because the photographer was unaware that the cassette slot is not absolutely light-tight.

The driver who uses his car only once a year cannot be a good driver. Equally we shall find it difficult and cumbersome to handle a camera when we take photographs only rarely. The best way of making progress is regular practice. To some extent we can do this without film; but although this method is cheap, it is also uncontrollable. 35 mm and medium-format negative film costs so little that we can practise even with real film in the camera without going to too much expense. The film need only be processed and after drying inspected with a magnifier or, better still, projected as a negative in a changing mount. If we view such a 35 mm negative at a projected size of 1 m (40 in), all technical defects which are far too insignificant in the usual 7 × 10 cm (3$^1/_4$ × 4$^1/_4$ in) enlargement will stand out prominently. Since we do not have positives made of the film, the cost remains low. We shall be surprised next time we are on holiday at our own skill in handling our camera, and at the rich harvest of successful snapshots because we have acquired the necessary dexterity.

Practice shots for the advanced worker, for instance, involve studies of how a person walks and when to press the button. We let a person walk across the field of view, counting left . . . right . . . and release the shutter when he

Top: This was not taken with the fisheye lens, so fashionable today. Almost the same effect was obtained with a Christmas Tree decoration.
Bottom: The long focal length (135 mm) made it possible to take this snapshot completely unnoticed. *Both photographs by Werner Köhler.*

puts down either the left or the right foot. This does not mean that from now on people should be photographed only in this position. But if we intend to record a certain position, we must be able to master the technique. From photographing correctly how a person walks to the competent sports picture is only a small step.

Here, too, it is vital to press the button at exactly the right phase. It is interesting to note that, e. g. with a high jump, the beginner almost invariably releases the shutter prematurely. Unless we are fully familiar with the type of sport we wish to photograph we had best ask an expert to indicate the photogenic position by a knock and try to catch it by pressing the button.

Owners of a system camera should now practise handling it with longer-focal-length lenses. Since it is impossible to refocus rapid movements, we are forced to use the opposite method of focusing first, letting the subject move into focus. Neither in the measuring viewfinder nor on the focusing screen can we ascertain the optimum sharpness during a movement. We must there-fore practise correlating the size a person standing still has in the viewfinder with his camera distance. When a runner, for instance, reaches this size in the viewfinder, it will be at the distance we have already determined for this size. It is only fair to say that a lot of practice film is necessary until we reach consistently reliable results.

A snapshot system

The first condition of a sound snapshot technique is efficient handling of the camera, which is speeded up by simplification. The three important controls are lens stop — shutter speed — distance setting. For many situations they can be set in advance. All we need to concentrate on then is the picture area and the right moment of releasing the shutter. In order to be ready for action the camera should be carried openly on the neck strap. For 23 DIN (160 ASA) black-and-white film the exposure should be

in sunlight: shutter speed $1/_{125}$ sec at f/11 or $1/_{250}$ sec at f/8

in good light without sun: shutter speed $1/_{125}$ sec at f/8.

It is advisable to set the distance exactly provided there is time for it. Failing this 3 standard settings will cover most of the ground. 5 m (17 ft) is the ideal value for all street scenes. At f/11 the depth of field will extend from 3 to

15 m (10–50 ft). If the background is pictorially important so that it must appear pin sharp it is best to focus on 10 m (33 ft), which will provide depth of field from 5 m (17 ft) to infinity. The third setting at 2.5 m (8 ft 6 in) opens up the near range from 2 m to 3.5 m (6 ft 8 in to 11 ft).

It is a great advantage to be able to visualize these distances of 2.5 m (8 ft 6 in), 5 m (17 ft), and 10 m (33 ft). Estimating them along the ground is more accurate than by direct sighting. If there is time, it is good practice first to estimate the distance of the pictorially important object, to measure it with the rangefinder, and to compare the value obtained with the estimate. With the longer focal lengths, which demand accurate distance settings, we can employ the following technique: We do not measure the object distance directly but that of another object equally far away. Our estimating ability is very good when we have a reference distance. Our point of view corresponds, as it were, to the apex of an isosceles triangle; one side is the distance measured, the other that of the object. At the suitable moment we swivel the camera round and press the button.

Practical tips

> The smaller the camera format, the more fully must we utilize it by approaching the subject as closely as we can; the main subject must appear as large in the field as possible.
> With close-up photography, we check the picture area with one eye; this reveals disturbing elements in the background at once.
> We must not stop down too much with close-ups of persons; otherwise restless features in the background become too obtrusive.
> When we take upright pictures, we must hold the flap of the ever-ready case back so that it does not obscure the field.
> We must not forget to pull out and lock collapsible lenses.
> The lens hood/filter combination can lead to vignetting if the distance between lens and lens hood is increased by the insertion of the filter.
> With a rangefinder camera we must remember that lens caps are opaque.
> It is advisable to take several exposures of an interesting subject (we must not forget to vary our viewpoint). This is far from being a waste.
> Even at $1/125$ sec some pictures will suffer from camera shake. When we are out of breath it is better to open up one stop and expose at $1/250$ sec.

> For exposures from moving trains or other vehicles the normal shutter speeds are $^1/_{250}$ or $^1/_{500}$ sec.

> The higher the speed of a lens (e.g. f/2 or f/1.4), the easier it is to use instantaneous shutter speeds in poor lighting conditions. The depth of field, however, is necessarily restricted. If we do not intend to work in this field of photography, the purchase of a camera with an f/2.8 lens will meet all our needs. The money we save thereby we can spend on a second lens of a different focal length if we own a system camera.

> The photographic term "infinity" is not identical with the mathematical concept. With high demands of quality and at full apertures, we can equate the following values with "infinity" distances for the 35 mm format at the various focal lengths:

Focal lengths of up to   35 mm — objects further away than   25 m (83 ft)
focal lengths of up to   50 mm — objects further away than   50 m (166 ft)
focal lengths of up to 100 mm — objects further away than 150 m (500 ft)
focal lengths of up to 135 mm — objects further away than 300 m (1000 ft)

> During the loading of a camera with a coupled exposure meter it is important to set the film speed on the exposure meter.

> The handling differs widely with the various camera models. A short check list of cues for using the camera should be made. It should begin with the loading of the film and end with the unloading of the exposed film.

> To remind ourselves, after a few days, of the type of film in our camera, we stick a self-adhesive label on the top of our camera, indicating type and speed of the film and number of exposures.

Exposure

Correct exposure is essential to a good result. We cannot rely on the estimating ability of our eye. If reference values are available the eye estimates very efficiently; without them, difficulties will arise at once. It is easy to determine exposures from experience in the summer sunlight; we shall immediately

Movement blur is one of the modern means of pictorial expression. In order to become really familiar with its effect, we make trial exposures at graded shutter speeds. The difference between a stationary camera and one that follows the subject is important.

Camera steady
¹/₅₀₀ sec

Camera steady
¹/₃₀ sec

Camera following
¹/₆₀ sec

Success depends on the right moment.

Merry antics on the beach. The worm's-eye view enhances the effect.

Taking photographs while you walk is very difficult. Never press the button at the instant of "putting your foot down".

Start photography demands some practice; it is easy to press the button too early.

Here you should count "left, right, left, right . . ." in order to catch the right phase of the movement. Guard in front of Buckingham Palace.
Leica M 3, 50 mm Summicron, f/5.6, $^{1}/_{250}$ sec, Isopan FF. Photograph by Walter Lueden.

From the stalls such pictures are not too difficult to take on ultra-high-speed film and with a fast lens if you go to see the same performance twice or if you do not skimp with film. Photograph by Kisselbach

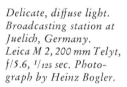

Different lighting contrast.

Delicate, diffuse light. Broadcasting station at Juelich, Germany. Leica M 2, 200 mm Telyt, f/5.6, ¹/125 sec. Photograph by Heinz Bogler.

Sunlight from the side. House front in Lisbon. Leica M 2, 125 mm Hektor, f/8, ¹/125 sec. Photograph by Robert Haeuser.

Stark contrast through contre-jour light. Steeplechase. Leicaflex, 135 mm Elmarit, ¹/1000 sec. Photograph by J. Makovec

be at a loss when we have to do it inside a church. The ability of our eyes to adapt themselves will compensate partially for the brightness difference. Most exposure estimates of interior subjects are too short.

The exposure meters, which measure the light quite objectively, are a great help. Since there is, however, quite a number of different systems available, they will be discussed in a special chapter. At this point only the basic conditions are of interest. Light from the sun or any other light source striking the object is reflected by it. This reflected light is decisive for the exposure time. It naturally has a certain relation to the incident light. This ratio varies as the object to be photographed is mainly white, e.g. a snowscape, or black, like a chimney sweep.

Our camera has individual narrow tolerances in the shutter speeds and in the lens apertures. The same applies to our exposure meter, and even the film and the method of development can deviate a little form the mean value without constituting an error. It is therefore urgently recommended to match these factors by means of a series of test exposures. We determine the exposure time with our exposure meter but begin our series two shutter speeds faster than the measured value suggests. We choose an architectural object in lateral sunlight.

Let us assume that the shutter speed measured at f/8 is $1/125$ sec for a 22 DIN — 125 ASA film: the exposure series will then read as follows: f/8 $1/500$ — $1/250$ — $1/125$ — $1/60$ — $1/30$ — $1/15$ sec. After processing, this film strip will show us how doubling the exposure each time affects the negative. At the same time we can check whether the measured $1/125$ sec is the correct mean value or we have to rate the film speed higher or lower.

The utilizable speed of a film can be influenced by the method of development (shorter or longer). Experimenting is not recommended here. A 36-exposure 35 mm film will very often contain negatives of the most varied subject contrasts. As long as we develop normally, further evaluation of the negatives will present no difficulties. Although with prolonged development we shall obtain a somewhat higher speed, and can therefore slightly reduce our exposure, we shall immediately run into difficulties with contrasty or contre jour subjects because the negatives will become too hard.

How to measure exposure correctly

The assumption or knowledge that his exposure meter — built into the camera or separate — is reliable leads many an owner to the conclusion that all his exposures must be correct. This conclusion should be valid once he has calibrated camera, exposure meter, and film (with black-and-white film also the developing method) in order to eliminate the small tolerances.

In reality a few imponderables remain; these are based on the fact that our photographic objects can have vastly different contrast ranges — the brightness differences between the brightest and the darkest portions of the subject. Our eye has the ability, when looking at a sunlit landscape from inside a room, to switch over instantly to the much greater brightness outside. It can accommodate without difficulty brightness differences of 1 : 500. The photographic emulsion is unable to do this. It is impossible to render both extremes correctly at the same time. We must decide: is the landscape to be rendered correctly, or is the interior more important, in which case we have to eliminate the influence of the bright landscape during the measurement.

The considerations apply also to the colour reversal film, although when this is projected a longer brightness range can be reproduced than on photographic paper.

In other cases, too, our measurement may be adversely affected if the brightness of the camera subject differs radically from that of the standard object (which reflects $1/6$ of the incident light). Pictures in the snow are the most frequent examples. If we assume a snowscape with more than 70% snow area, this will reflect more than 68% of the light, not the 17% of the standard object. Our exposure meter therefore indicates 2 lens stops smaller than at an intensity of illumination in normal conditions.

Now it is true that we can use less exposure for snow than for a standard object, but only by 1 lens stop, and not by the 2 indicated by the exposure meter. If our exposure meter reads, e.g. f/11 — $1/250$ sec, we expose f/11 — $1/125$ sec or f/8 $1/250$ sec. Snowscapes with only 40% snow area are correctly exposed at the value indicated.

With night pictures the situation is exactly reversed if only small parts of the picture are intensely illuminated and the surrounding field is in darkness.

The correction must now be towards less exposure. If we are able to approach the object closely enough to establish normal conditions within the measuring angle, the measurement will be at once correct.

In order to understand the function of a photo-electric exposure meter we must be familiar with the basic conditions governing the measurement. The camera subject reflects only a part of the light incident upon it. For average objects this proportion is laid down as $1/6$. The incident light is measured in lux (lx), the reflected light in apostilb (asb).

If all the light reflected at a certain angle is utilized for the measurement we speak of integrated (or area) measurement. With the vast majority of subjects this type of measurement produces correct exposures. Since the contrast of our objects can, however, vary enormously (contre jour, view of a sunlit landscape from inside a room, etc.) this measuring technique demands close-up readings in difficult cases or minor corrections of the normal reading. It has therefore been variously suggested to measure the incident instead of the reflected light, i.e. the intensity of the illumination, because this makes it easier to standardize the corrections. This, however, would require a close approach to the camera subject, which is very often impossible.

This form of light measurement has therefore been replaced during recent years by measurement within a comparatively narrow angle of field, which means that instead of the whole object only a characteristic part of it is used for the measurement. In our view from a room we measure the brightness of the landscape or, if only the room is pictorially important, that of the room to obtain the correct exposure time in each instance. The earlier measurement integrating indoors and outdoors produced a wrong value.

Exposure measurement in close-up photography. Unless our camera offers through-the-lens metering we must, with close-up objects, consider the measuring angle of the exposure meter. We approach the object close enough so that we cover, if possible, only the portion important to the exposure, without casting our own shadow across it. If the brightness of the object is very uneven, it is best to take the exposure reading off a piece of medium grey cardboard.

Selenium-cell exposure meters

In a selenium-cell exposure meter the incident light directly generates an electric current, which increases corresponding to the intensity of the incident light. This is measured directly with a built-in measuring instrument. Provided sufficient light is available, the performance of selenium-cell exposure meters is very satisfactory. Since, however, they are much less light-sensitive and much larger than the CdS exposure meters described below, they are losing more and more ground.

CdS exposure meters

The light-sensitive cell of this type of meter is a cadmium sulphide photo-resistor. Unlike the selenium cell it does not generate a current, but changes its resistance according to the quantity of incident light. Its current source is a mercuric oxide battery (Mallory PX 13), which has an average life of 1–2 years. If much light reaches the photo-resistor this transmits much, if little light reaches it, little current from the battery. Most cameras incorporate a control device with which the potential of the battery can be tested. The measuring instrument in the circuit supplies the value of the brightness. The most outstanding advantage of the CdS exposure meter is its light sensitivity, which is much superior to that of the selenium cell exposure meter. This enables us to use much narrower acceptance angles for the measurement. There is a slight difference between the spectral sensitivity of the film and that of the CdS photo-resistor, which has a somewhat lower blue and a somewhat higher red sensitivity. Whereas the photo-resistor is little affected by temperature, the battery is sensitive to cold, and repeated checks with the battery tester at low temperatures are recommended. CdS photo-resistors have a memory. They show deviations if we want to measure very high and very low intensities of illumination (bright landscapes, dark interiors) in quick succession. They therefore require a few minutes to adapt themselves.
Their high limiting sensitivity and small size have made the design of cameras possible in which the CdS exposure meter measures the light through the lens. Since the structural details vary a great deal, we must carefully study the operating instructions for the camera. Exposure meters with measuring instruments are sensitive to shock and impact, because the latter are suspended between very fine points.

If the lighting contrast is strong as in this outside view from inside a room you must decide which is more important, the interior or the landscape, because integrated light measurement (sum total of the reflected light) produces wrong results here.

For the top picture the measurement ignored the window, for the bottom picture, however, it was taken near the window.

The grey oblong below corresponds roughly to the "average object" of 17 % reflection, for which the exposure meters are calibrated.

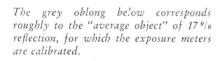

Decisive for the exposure time is the landscape without the dark tree trunks to the left and right. Depending on the measuring angle of the exposure meter several methods are used to obtain the correct exposure. With a hand-held meter, or with a built-in exposure meter accepting a wide measuring angle, walk a few paces forward, take the reading, return to your previous position, and expose. This procedure is unnecessary if you are the owner of an exposure meter working at a narrow measuring angle, which does not take in the dark surrounding field.

The correct exposure of this ice skater will be obtained only if the dark surroundings are excluded from the measurement. Either approach your subject very closely or use an exposure meter of suitably narrow measuring angle.

Photographs by Kisselbach

Snow pictures

Faulty measurements are very common here, because the abundance of white leads to the assumption that the exposure could be reduced. Actually the exposure meter does measure this enormous quantity of light.

The top picture, for instance, was exposed at one lens stop larger than indicated by the meter. Photograph by Prof. Hoppichler

The bottom picture, on the other hand, calls for no correction, because here the shadows and the dark pine trees balance the measurement.

Photograph by Julius Behnke

Pouring out the famous Frankfurt cider. There was much less light present than the picture suggests. Even screened household lamps are powerful enough for a shutter speed of ¹/₃₀ sec on ultra-high-speed film (400 ASA, 27 DIN) and with the 50 mm Summilux f/1.4 at full aperture. Since in these conditions exposure measurement is often difficult, point the exposure meter at your palm held in an area decisive for the exposure. Leica M 4, photograph by Guenter Osterloh.

The automatic camera

It has for long been the wish of many amateurs to be able to take photographs with as few problems and as quickly as possible. The conception of automation here refers only to automatic exposure control. The first versions have mechanical, programme-controlled shutters. In practice, automatic exposure controls of this kind have been found very reliable when meeting average demands. They are most convenient for photography outdoors and on holidays.

Their limitations become evident only when we want to work in certain fields such as sports, interiors in poor lighting conditions, and any branches stretching photographic possibilities to the limit. These limitations depend on the type of the exposure control.

We are sometimes restricted to certain shutter speed/stop combinations; with a sports subject, for instance, we cannot choose a shutter speed of $1/500$ sec at full aperture, simply because the highest shutter speed is programmed with small aperture stops. With some cameras we do not know the stop/shutter speed combinations we are using at all, because there is only a red/green indication, red meaning "not enough light for an instantaneous exposure", green "exposure possible".

Some cameras in which the use of electronic components in the shutter and of ultra-sensitive CdS measuring cells has enlarged the range of applications tremendously have now reached the market. Lens stop and shutter speed are simultaneously indicated in the viewfinder. When we rotate the diaphragm ring the shutter speed will be correspondingly adjusted.

The automation, then, consists in the shutter speed being set automatically to a preselected lens stop. If we want to take a picture at $1/500$ sec we rotate the diaphragm ring until the figure 500 appears in the viewfinder. Conversely, if we need a great depth of field, we can set a small lens stop and read the corresponding shutter speed in the viewfinder. With fixed camera lenses functional reliability of the automatic device can be achieved by a design less complicated than where the lens is interchangeable. It is most important that with automatic cameras incorporating electric batteries a reserve battery should always be at hand — no current, no automation.

The advantage of automation is, however, strictly confined to the field of exposure. What we want to photograph, and what camera position we want to use continues to be a matter of our personal choice.

Light measurement through the lens (TTL-measuring system)

The very high light sensitivity of the CdS photo-resistors permits the design of exposure meters which measure the light in the camera body behind the lens. This offers a number of advantages, especially with system cameras with interchangeable lenses, because it enables us to measure the light exactly within the angle of field of the taking lens.

The first models using the TTL system were 35 mm single-lens-reflex cameras. The most favourable measuring site would be the film plane. Since we are unable to measure there, the focusing plane or its vicinity has been chosen in most such cameras. Unfortunately stray light from the observation eyepiece can influence the measurement there. The most varied optical or mechanical blocks are used to eliminate this. Most cameras employ the principle of integrated (area) measurement, i.e. they measure the sum total of the light coming from the object. A photographic subject displays a whole range of brightnesses. So long as very bright or very dark portions do not predominate or the brightness difference between them is not extremely great, integration will be satisfactory, and the exposure measurement produce the correct results. This method is very simple to use in practice, but cannot solve all exposure problems.

How can we overcome the disadvantages of integrated measurement in difficult lighting conditions? By narrowing the measuring field to an area large enough for a characteristic feature to be measured without difficulty, but small enough for the usual disturbing factors to be eliminated. This requires an integrated measurement of a characteristic feature, and is called selective (or detail, or spot) measurement. It is not as straightforward as the pure integrated measurement.

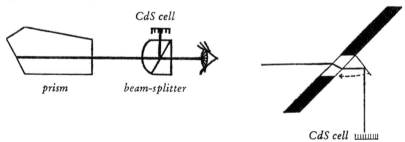

Part of the incident light is deflected to the CdS cell through the beam splitter (left) or the semi-transparent mirror (right).

System cameras

With a system camera we can combine the various components into a wide range of different assemblies like a construction set. The nucleus is the camera body with the standard-focal-length lens, which can be taken out and replaced by one of longer or shorter focal length. We can cover quite different angles of view from the same camera position and thereby different picture areas at different reproduction scales. Further accessories open up the close-up range; this, too, can be achieved not just with one lens, but with several lenses of different focal lengths.

On the other hand it is also possible to work with several camera bodies or magazines with different films, e. g. black-and-white and colour.

Most system cameras have been designed for the 24×36 mm (35 mm) and for the 6×6 cm ($2^{1}/_{4} \times 2^{1}/_{4}$ in) format. In the 35 mm format the range of focal-length variations is wider, and the accessories and attachments are more numerous. Camera systems in the 6×6 cm ($2^{1}/_{4} \times 2^{1}/_{4}$ in) format are more expensive, because the corresponding focal lengths must always be 50% longer than in the 35 mm format.

The possibilities of variation are so vast and we can combine so many special outfits for particular tasks, that only few of us will be able to exhaust the entire range available. Nor can it be the ultimate aim of the owner of a system camera to possess as many accessories as possible, but only those actually necessary for the field he is interested in. Even two or three lenses expand the camera range appreciably.

We can exhaust the technical potentialities only if our mastery of the various components is complete. Their ownership alone does not lead to achievement. The obvious step after we buy a new accessory should therefore be that we learn how to use it by practice exposures. The cost of the practice films is generally the most insignificant item on the shopping list.

The various accessories are known by technical terms with whose significance we should be familiar:

Standard focal length: the focal length of a camera lens corresponding roughly to or slightly varying from the diagonal of the film format; i.e. $42-60$ mm for the 35 mm format, $75-80$ mm for the 6×6 cm ($2^{1}/_{4} \times 2^{1}/_{4}$ in) format. The fastest lenses of a system are offered in the standard focal length.

The computation of ultra-fast lenses is no longer as difficult as it used to be. Practice, however, imposes a number of limitations, caused by the imperfect planeness of the film and the progressively shallower depth of field. With 35 mm film, apertures of up to f/1.4 can be used; but f/2.8 must be considered the limit for 6 × 6 cm (2¹/₄ × 2¹/₄ in) because of the slightly less plane position of the film in the camera.

Wide-angle lenses have focal lengths shorter than the film diagonal. New scientific progress has made the computation of very extreme angles of field possible. There is, however, a basic distinction between systems that are free from appreciable distortion and the so-called *fisheye cameras*, which produce pictures resembling the reflections seen on Christmas tree decorations.

Wide-angle lenses produce great depth of field, and are therefore often recommended as snapshot lenses. We achieve good pictorial effects if the main subject occupies the foreground. Wide-angle lenses are also indispensable for architectural photography, both interior and exterior.

Back focus (retro-focus) lenses are optical systems of increased intercept distance. Since space is required for the unobstructed movement of the mirror in single-lens-reflex cameras, the design especially of wide-angle lenses must be modified. The rearmost member must be further away from the film than in normal conditions. This is achieved by the incorporation of one or two large negative members in the first element. The optical design is therefore vastly more complicated than in a wide-angle lens of conventional construction. The most outstanding advantage is little vignetting.

All wide-angle lenses make focusing difficult with 35 mm single-lens-reflex cameras, because the details on the focusing screen appear so tiny that the eye has difficulty in differentiating them. We can guess distances above 2 m (6 ft 8 in) quite successfully and focus the lens accordingly.

Wide-angle lenses with adjustable axis. When the camera is tilted, converging verticals will be produced. We can avoid them by moving the lens to one side from the centre of its rigid mount; similar to operating the cross front of the

Lenses of different focal lengths at a given camera position produce images of different sizes. At the same time the picture area correspondingly varies.
p. 73: Group of apostles by Tilman Riemenschneider, State Museum, Berlin-Dahlem.
pp. 74/75: Stork's nest, Atzbach, nr. Wetzlar. All photographs by Kisselbach.

▼ 50 mm   ▲ 35 mm   ▼ 135 mm

▼ 200 mm   ▲ 400 mm   ▼ 90 mm   ▶ 21 mm

large-format camera. Lens designs which meet this requirement have now been developed for single-lens-reflex cameras. We see the effect directly on the focusing screen.

Their advantage is most noticeable with colour reversal film, because here correction of converging verticals is not possible. In the normal position the lenses can be used for all conventional wide-angle subjects. Since their optical and mechanical design is very complicated, this type of wide-angle lens is considerably more expensive than the ordinary version.

Long-focal-length and telephoto lenses are systems of longer focal lengths. The difference between the two types of lens consists in that the overall length of long-focal-length lenses corresponds to their focal length, whereas the overall length and intercept distance of telephoto lenses is shorter in relation to their focal length. The optical performance of telephoto lenses is almost as good as that of the long-focal-length variety except that it falls off more rapidly in the near-focusing range. But since in the interest of sufficient depth of field we must almost invariably stop down, here, too, the difference is not very significant.

From 100 mm focal length upwards the use of the mirror reflex system for focusing has increasing advantages in the 35 mm format.

For single-lens-reflex cameras telephoto lenses are preferred, because the automatic diaphragm mechanism can be designed much more efficiently when the diaphragm is located nearer to the lens. Operation does not appreciably differ whether we use a long-focal-length- or a telephoto lens in the camera. The narrower angle of field offers many advantages in pictorial composition. Likewise the shallow depth of field is useful because the clear-cut transition from sharpness to unsharpness provides good spatial orientation.

Catoptric (mirror) lenses are special lenses of very long focal length and very short overall length. However, they cannot be stopped down; their light transmission can be reduced only with grey filters.

Vario lenses, also called zoom lenses, are systems of variable focal lengths. Their optical design (a total of 12—20 members depending on the type)

The fields covered by lenses of different focal lengths outlined here provide a rough survey how much or how little is reproduced from a given camera position. In practice the photographer will try to make his subject fill the frame by adapting his camera position to the focal length of the lens in his camera. Wetzlar Cathedral. Leica M 3, 21 mm Super-Angulon. Photograph by R. Seck.

requires a basic lens with a variator in front. With some systems the variation of the focal length (the zoom range) is 1 : 2, 1 : 4, and even greater. The maximum aperture is f/2.8 or f/4.

The effective light transmission of zoom lenses is almost half a stop less than that of conventional ones, because in spite of lens coating the losses owing to reflection and absorption are more noticeable with the many members than with the usual 5 or 6. Although the optical performance is not quite equal to that of the lenses of fixed focal length, the difference has now become so small that during projection of colour reversal film it becomes evident only from the shortest viewing distance. The great advantage of such zoom systems is that they offer a continuous range of intermediate focal lengths, which makes it vastly easier to fill the frame with the subject. This is particularly important with colour reversal film.

Converter. This is a simple optical attachment for single-lens-reflex cameras. It is a negative system comprising 3 or 4 members, which is inserted between camera body and lens. Ordinary versions double the focal length of the lens with which they are used. Doubling the focal length reduces the lens speed by 2 stops. The speed value engraved on the basic lens, e.g. f/4, in reality corresponds to f/8. Since the optical performance is somewhat impaired by the converter, we must stop the lens down further. This loss of speed considerably restricts its practical uses.

Half binoculars. This system, which is occasionally recommended as a telephoto lens attachment, also has its limitations. If we use one half of an 8 × 30 glass, the lens speed will be about f/16. With a standard focal length of 50 mm and the 8 × magnification of the binoculars, the taking focal length will be 400 mm. Unfortunately, definition and brilliance in no way match that of a simple achromat of 400 mm focal length stopped down to f/16.

Anamorphic lenses are used in cinematography in order to obtain wide-screen effects with ordinary cameras and projectors. These attachments have been available for single-lens-reflex cameras for some time now. The anamorphic lens includes a cylindrical lens system which changes the height/width relationship at a ratio of 1 : 1.5. This produces a pronounced panoramic effect in horizontal pictures. In order to obtain the wide-screen effect in projection, the attachment is used once again; it is necessary to adapt the projection screen to the new side ratio 1 : 2.25.

Changing the perspective and the spatial effect

Lenses of different focal lengths, although they reproduce objects at different sizes from a given camera position, leave the perspective unchanged. With a longer focal length the picture area will be correspondingly smaller, but the reproduction would be the same if we enlarged the object from a shorter-focal-length rendering. The only evident difference is the lower resolving power of the much enlarged picture and the consequent loss of detail (focal length comparison see examples pp. 73–75).

It is, however, possible to change the camera position as we change the lens, so that some parts of the subject will have the same size in both pictures. The size relationship between parts of the subject in the foreground and in the background is radically changed with the various focal lengths and a change in the camera position, particularly when we try to fill the frame with our subject also with the shorter focal lengths. If no lenses of different focal lengths are available we can imagine the effect by looking through a 5 × 5 cm (2 × 2 in) frame (p. 18). An example of different perspective will be found on pp. 82 and 83.

Wide-angle lenses emphasize the foreground. Lines leading into the picture converge very rapidly and enhance the impression of depth. But details in the background are reproduced very small because of the relatively short focal length of these lenses. In certain conditions the wide angle of field will include very many details which because of their abundance and minute reproduction have a restless effect.

Longer-focal-length lenses, owing to their narrower angle of field, cover only a limited area. The shallow depth of field differentiates the space more strikingly. Objects in the background are rendered at sufficient size. Since the field includes only a few lines and shapes, these can be better composed in space. To the users of the 35 mm format the focal lengths from 25 to 150 mm will be of interest. They normally allow hand-held exposures without difficulty. The use of more extreme focal lengths at either end of this range calls for more photographic experience.

It is very important and useful to realize the different effects of different focal lengths by means of a series of comparison pictures. The successive focal lengths should differ by the factor 2 or 3.

Large-format cameras with a wide range of movements

The large format begins at 9 × 12 cm (¼-plate). This and larger formats are used preferably in professional photography, where the many camera movements are very handy in certain situations. This advantage of adaptation also requires more technical skill.

There are two fundamentally different systems: the one based on the old folding camera with pull-out lens panel and multiple extension, and the other built on the principle of the optical bank.

The following movements are available: the lens panel provides for the interchange of lenses, usually with their own between-lens shutter. The lens can be vertically (rise and drop front) and laterally (cross front) adjusted and sometimes tilted or rotated. The frame with the focusing screen is mounted in the camera back. Here, too, movements are provided. Back and lens panel are joined by means of a lightproof bellows. In order to match the various movements correctly it is necessary to check the sharpness conditions on the focusing screen with the greatest care. This is done with the aid of a magnifier under a black focusing cloth.

For the actual exposure we almost invariably stop down both when the utmost precision in sharpness must be obtained and when a great depth of field is required. Since the scale of subsequent enlargement is much reduced, even very small lens stops can be used.

With large-format cameras the cost of the exposure material will loom quite large in our budget. But since we shall become proficient workers only with practice, it is a good idea to insert a piece of "soft" bromide paper instead of the large, expensive sheet films in the darkslide for this purpose. This paper is considerably slower than the film, and a short test is necessary to allow for this (step exposure by a step-by-step adjustment of the darkslide cover). A paper negative is eminently suitable for a check whether the movements were handled correctly (the bromide paper must be trimmed to exactly the right size).

In narrow palace yards the camera must be tilted upwards if it has no rising front. Those specializing in architectural photography will in certain conditions depend on a camera with all the movements. Weilburg Castle. Photograph by Kisselbach.

The pictures on the left, taken in the park of Nymphenburg Palace near Munich, were produced with lenses of two different focal lengths. Top 35 mm, bottom 90 mm.

The camera position was moved to the rear until the stone vase in the foreground appeared at the same size as in the 35 mm picture.

The background is pulled in by the longer-focal-length lens. Photographs by Kisselbach

The pictures on the facing page were similarly varied. Mehrenburg Castle, top 90mm, bottom 35 mm lens. Photographs by Julius Behnke

Useful accessories

Lens hood. Its purpose is to prevent sunlight from entering the camera lens directly with contre-jour subjects. It is equally useful during rain, because raindrops on the front lens are even more disturbing. When the camera lens consists of many elements, any glaring surroundings should be masked, because they produce reflections. A lens hood is therefore never out of place.

The lens hood should be deep enough to afford sufficient protection without vignetting the corners of the subject. This may occur if the effective depth of the lens hood is increased by the insertion of a filter between it and the lens. Lens hoods made of rubber are very convenient and warmly recommended, although they will not last as long as metal ones.

Cable release. When the camera is mounted on a tripod, a cable release should be used to operate the shutter. Various types are available. For camera shutters without "T" setting, the cable release must have a clamping screw. The longer cable releases are better, because they reduce the risk of transmitting jerks etc. to the camera during long exposure times.

A twin cable release is used for special purposes, such as the simultaneous release of two cameras for stereo pictures or the operation of the automatic diaphragm and the shutter in single-lens-reflex cameras. The action of one of the releases is adjustable, so that it acts before the other.

Remote release. In animal photography it is often necessary to release the shutter from a long distance. By means of a thin rubber tube (System Rowi) we can bridge distances of up to about 30 m (100 ft). Cable connections and magnet releases are suitable for even longer distances.

Tripods are available in the most varied designs. They are used with shutter speeds slower than $^1/_{30}$ sec, to ensure that there is no camera shake. The particularly sturdy models used for larger cameras are also recommended for 35 mm cameras with long-focal-length lenses. Many have an adjustable centre column. It should not be extended fully as this reduces the stability of the tripod.

Worm's and bird's eye views. View upwards and downwards. Especially wide-angle lenses produce interesting perspective foreshortening. Top: Parthenon, Athens; bottom: View from the Eiffel Tower. Both photographs by Kisselbach.

Large tripods are cumbersome when we are travelling. There is little point in taking a smaller and lighter model along if its joints are not absolutely rigid. Here a *table tripod*, which has only three short legs and can be propped against a wall or set up on a table is much better.

Shoulder stocks, chainpods, unipods and similar aids are not designed for long time exposures, but only for improving steadiness of the camera with long-focal-length lenses. A good ball-and-socket head is essential with a good tripod. To ensure the necessary rigidity it should not be too light.

With very long focal lengths (400 mm and longer) we may in certain conditions not be able to obtain a steady camera release with the tripod alone. A second support should be used with stationary subjects.

Pistol grips. In connection with long-focal-length lenses, focusing bellows, and similar devices, the use of screw-on handgrips is very popular.

Self timer. Unless this is built into the camera, an attachable self timer must be used. Many photographers, however, prefer the pneumatic remote release already described, because this allows them to determine the moment of shutter release themselves.

Soft-focus discs with concentric rings are better than other versions, because they refract part of the rays in front and to the rear of the focusing plane. This produces not only an enhanced soft-focus effect, but also increased depth of field. The delicately balanced unsharpness imparts a certain "bloom" to the subject. The slightly softer rendering is popular in portraiture because it suppresses minor skin blemishes. The lighting should be arranged a little more contrasty than normal. White portions of the picture and highlights on metal will produce an attractive sparkle.

If you want to experiment with soft-focus discs in portraiture, here is a method tried by Windisch: place a star-shaped black paper mask between a yellow filter and a + 6 dioptre spectacle lens. The star-shaped mask does not altogether cut off the marginal rays, which are important to the soft-focus effect. This monocle lens is used in place of a camera lens in a single-lens-reflex camera with focusing bellows.

Front lens attachments are positive lenses which make the formation of a sharp image in the close-up range possible. Their use is very simple on single-lens-reflex cameras, because we can see their effect on the focusing screen. We must stop down to at least f/8, or better still to f/16 if possible.

If we want to use front lens attachments on cameras that do not allow any focusing control, we must carry out a sharpness test by photographing a cm scale at an angle of 45 °. The front lens attachment is focused on the middle portion of the scale according to the operating instructions supplied with it. The camera lens is focused on infinity. The processed negative will reveal whether the sharpness lies at the focused distance or not. Every centimetre on the scale represents a real distance of 7 mm. At this accurately determined distance, to be set most easily with a roller tape measure, the operation will be very reliable.

Correction lenses are mounted on the viewfinder eyelens to correct visual defects. Many people suffer from slight defects without wearing spectacles. The optical data for correction lenses must be based on the prescription for distance glasses. Sufferers from astigmatism should definitely wear spectacles, because the cylindrical lenses adapt themselves automatically with upright or horizontal camera positions. Otherwise the correction lenses would have to be rotatable.

Extension rings increase the camera extension, thereby permitting close-up photography. See also the relevant chapter.

Underwater housing. Waterproof and pressure resistant housings are available for many cameras. The controls are usually operated from outside by means of rod linkages. The camera technique requires very thorough experience not only in the photographic field, but also in diving. Colour photographs are particularly striking. Even at a depth of only a few m, the sun's rays contain only blue light; most colour photographs are therefore taken with flash.

Camera cases. Ever-ready cases are offered for many cameras. Unfortunately most of them interfere with instant readiness for action. If we are keen on snapshots, it will be better to carry the camera on a strap, because all the buttons and levers will then be readily accessible. For transport we put the camera with accessories into an oblong camera case.

*

Many other accessories exist for scientific purposes, reportage, advertising photography, nature observation, and other special fields. Your photo-dealer will be pleased to advise you on problems that will arise here.

BLACK-AND-WHITE FILMS

Properties

Within the last few years the proportion of black-and-white photography has been continuously shrinking. Nevertheless, black-and-white films are very important for many purposes, and so valuable to the understanding of the photographic problems that they will always take up a considerable proportion of photographic consumption. We should be familiar with the properties of the black-and-white films in order to use them correctly. Since films are affected by storage, an expiry date is printed on the container. We can assume the date of manufacture to be 2−2¹/₂ years earlier. Correct storage, preferably in a cool and dry place, is important. A plastic bag in the vegetable compartment of the refrigerator is best.

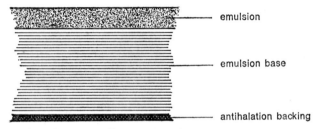

Enlarged cross section through a 35 mm film (not to scale).

General sensitivity

Among the properties of a film its general sensitivity is decisive because it governs its exposure time. In Germany the sensitivity, in short film speed, is stated in DIN degrees. The graduation has been chosen so that an increase of 3 DIN means double the speed, and a decrease of 3 DIN half the speed of a given DIN value. Manufacturing tolerance is only 1 DIN. The speed is measured according to a procedure laid down precisely by a DIN specification. The utilizable speed can be changed by means of the method of development. A speed reserve of 3 DIN is normal. When a "magic developer" claims a higher speed utilization, it will be of interest only if this is more than 3 DIN. In ordinary work it is not advisable to use up this speed reserve,

Comparison of the soft, normal, and hard gradations.

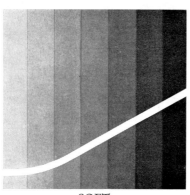

SOFT

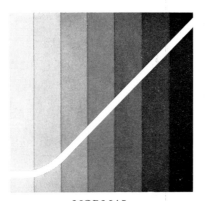

NORMAL

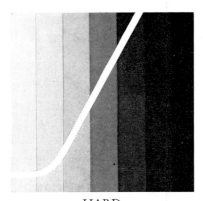

HARD

GREEN ▶   ◀ BLUE

GREY ▶   ◀ RED

Different grey values of the colours depending on the sensitization (colour sensitivity) of the exposure material.
unsensitized (ordinary)

orthochromatic

panchromatic

The films obtainable today are almost all panchromatic. Orthochromatic or ordinary films will be used only in special cases.

Influence of the exposure on the resolving power of the film.

n sein H
ührung v
her impu
dem Photo
Photofac

To demonstrate the difference, 40 x part-enlargements were made, i.e. a 35 mm film was enlarged to 96 x 144 cm (approx. 38 x 58 in). Type and graph paper are particularly critical objects.

.n sein H
ührung v
her impu
dem Photo
Photofac

With correct exposure both negative and positive approximately correspond to the original. With increasing exposure — twice or four times as long — the quality deteriorates owing to halation. Further deterioration is caused by excessive development of the film.

n sein H
ührung v
her impu
dem Photo
Photofac

The thinner the emulsion layer and the better the antihalation protection, the less evident will these disturbances be.

n sein H
ührung v
her impu
dem Photo
Photofac

because it is automatically compensated by minor variations of the exposure meter. Only if we are forced by unfavourable conditions to go to the limit of under-exposure are we justified in taking up this latitude.

The American speed rating ASA is internationally known. To all intents and purposes it coincides with the British BS system although it has a different theoretical basis. Here, twice a given value indicates twice the speed. Easily memorized comparative values are 12 DIN = 12 ASA, 21 DIN = 100 ASA.

Colour sensitivity

Even though a black-and-white film translates colours only into grey values, we still speak of its colour sensitivity. The photographic emulsion is inherently sensitive to the ultraviolet to blue wave lengths. Through the addition of dyes during the manufacture of the emulsion this sensitivity is extended to other colours. The panchromatic films in common use today have a sensitivity extending to red.

The beginner will not find it easy to visualize this translation of colours into grey steps. Colour contrasts as strong as green and red may in certain conditions result in almost identical grey values. It is therefore generally recommended to pay more attention to the lighting contrast, where the difference will always persist. The chapter on filters contains examples how to influence

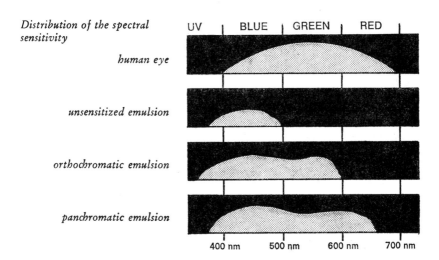

Distribution of the spectral sensitivity

UV | BLUE | GREEN | RED

human eye

unsensitized emulsion

orthochromatic emulsion

panchromatic emulsion

400 nm   500 nm   600 nm   700 nm

◀ *Kalvarienberg, Bad Tölz. Orange filter. Photograph by Theo M. Scheerer.*   93

the colour rendering. So-called ordinary, non-sensitized films, responding only to the ultraviolet to blue light, are today used only for special purposes. Likewise, "orthochromatic" films will also be used exceptionally only. The latter films are sensitive to green and yellow, but not to red.

Gradation

In ordinary photography we need emulsions that reproduce perfectly all brightness steps from the brightest white to the deepest black. These films are of normal gradation. This can, however, be influenced by the duration of the development. The shorter the development, the flatter the gradation. Very long development produces contrasty negatives.

A film of soft gradation reduces the steps between the individual tone values and can therefore accommodate greater light contrasts. A film of hard gradation, on the other hand, enhances small brightness differences, making objects poor in contrast appear brilliant. But it is unable to reproduce great brightness contrasts in correct tone values.

For the scientific classification of the gradation we enter the density values on graph paper according to the logarithmic progression. Since the amateur lacks the facilities for the densitometric evaluation of his photographs, the conventional indications of the gamma values are only of theoretical significance to him. The practitioner interested in this field will find it more useful to photograph a grey scale in standard conditions and to judge the various tone gradations according to this "standard object".

Resolving power and grain

Under the microscope the developed film reveals an irregular structure. This is caused by the irregular clumping together of neighbouring particles of metallic silver, to which the silver bromide crystals were reduced during development. The larger the original crystals and the more vigorous the developing process, the larger the conglomerations. The thickness of the emulsion layer, too, is of importance. A certain relationship exists between the sensitivity and the size of the silver bromide crystals. Ultra-fast emulsions thus have a coarser structure than slow ones. The manufacturing process, too, has a bearing on grain size, so that a faster film manufactured by A may have a finer structure than a slower film made by B.

94

The so-called resolving power of a film is its ability to differentiate between adjacent details. The graininess of the film has a considerable influence on resolving power.

The grain may be visible in a strip of film to a greater or lesser extent. The cause of this must be sought in the object contrast of the photographic motif. Uniform areas reveal more grain structure than well-differentiated portions. Grain is more noticeable in ultra-fast films with generous than with normal exposure.

If we want to use extremely fine-grain emulsions in order to eliminate all grain structure even at high enlarging scales, the use of so-called document-copying film is recommended. It is, however, very slow and its gradation very steep; by suitable precautions during development contrast can be reduced.

Freedom from halation and contour sharpness (acutance)

Our photographic emulsions are turbid media. If high light contrasts are recorded in a film, lateral scatter (halation) of the light will occur, e.g. around a light source. This scatter can never be completely eliminated, but it will be strongly reduced if measures are taken during the manufacture of the film so that reflection is not added to diffusion. These may consist in dyeing the photographic emulsion or the emulsion base, dyeing the back, and introduction of an intermediate layer between the photographic emulsion and its base. Correct exposure reduces, overexposure emphasizes halation.

Contour sharpness (acutance) is an objective measure of the sharpness properties of a film. Here the diffusion halo has a decisive influence. Contour sharpness is determined by means of a slit of $15/1000$ mm width, which is placed in contact with the film, and through which the film is exposed. The spread of the slit image on the processed negative is measured, and gives a comparable value. The emulsion thickness of the film has a considerable effect.

The film material

The photographic industry supplies films and plates some of which are for universal use; others are designed for special applications.

For a holiday trip we shall use a universal film of medium speed, which is sensitive enough for landscapes, street scenes, and light interiors. Although it is not extremely fast, nor is its resolving power the highest, the sum total of its properties offers the greatest latitude. A snapshot in the big city at night on the other hand demands an ultra-fast film. For the reproduction of a manuscript on yellowed paper, again, contrasty document copying film will have to be used, which is able to make even slight differences in contrast clearly stand out. It is true that with special negative development we can slightly adapt even universal emulsions to extreme tasks, but for economical methods with reliable results films of special properties are to be preferred. The following survey concentrates on film, because the production of photographic plates is all but a thing of the past. If a certain emulsion is still available in plate form, the information given below applies analogously.

General sensitivity is regarded, not always rightly, as the dominating property. But we, too, initially base our classification on the speed groups.

Ultra-fast film (200 ASA, 24 DIN)

Special film for poor lighting conditions. Any increase in speed improves the possibility of instantaneous exposure even in unfavourable light, as well as the range of cameras with lenses of small aperture.

Not recommended for good light on the beach, in snow, for distant views.

Particularly suitable for: bad weather, rain, blizzards, sport in artificial light, reportage in poor light, street scenes at night, pictures at home without flash, theatre, variety shows, circus, cinema.

Ultra-fast films are grainier than slow ones. They produce good results only with accurate (short rather than generous) exposure. Overexposure considerably increases the grain and reduces the resolving power. Grain is most disturbing in large, uniform, bright areas. With the 35 mm format, we utilize the entire frame for the subject.

The *gradation* of ultra-fast films today is normal to vigorous; in the past it was mostly soft. Developing times must be checked. For 35 mm film fine-grain or ultra-fine-grain developer is recommended. If possible we develop the film in complete darkness.

Normal or medium-speed films (17—23 DIN, 40—160 ASA)

Universal films, most favourable sum total of all the properties. Almost always fast enough for normal daylight. Higher resolving power than ultra-fast film. Little grain making part-enlargements possible. The wide exposure latitude of these films should not be fully utilized; correctly exposed negatives are easier to print.

Attention. In spite of the same speed rating various brands can have different properties.

SLOW FILMS (UP TO 16 DIN, 32 ASA)

Special films for extreme enlargements of 35 mm negatives. Available as roll film from only a few manufacturers. Very high resolving power and thin-film emulsion ensure finest detail rendering without disturbing grain structure. Thin-film emulsion demands accurate exposure. When in doubt, we take a series of different exposures until we are familiar with the material. The slow speed requires slower shutter speeds, which increases the risk of camera shake. Where maximum sharpness is essential a tripod will often have to be used.

DOCUMENT-COPYING FILMS

Document-copying films, originally made only for the reproduction of line originals, are today used by 35 mm workers also for pictorial photography. They are available as sheet film, plates, and 35 mm film (in bulk), but not as roll film, and in three types differing in their colour sensitivity (ordinary — orthochromatic — panchromatic).

Properties: The films have maximum resolving power and extremely fine grain. No rated speed is given, which makes correct exposure difficult. Basis for exposure meters about 10—13 DIN (8—16 ASA). The correct exposure depends on the method of development and must be matched to it. Exposure latitude is narrowest with contrasty development.

Uses
1) Line reproductions (pencil)
2) yellowed documents
3) pictures in fog
4) half-tone reproductions
5) landscapes
6) photomicrography.

Development is always individual and must be adapted to the subject. It therefore requires a certain amount of experience. Developers that can be well adapted to soft development, such as Rodinal 1 : 50, produce the best results.

Results will be astonishing once we are familiar with the material, but the narrow processing latitude calls for painstaking working procedures.

Negative materials for special purposes

In addition to the films listed so far a large number of exposure materials for technical and scientific purposes are available which cannot be readily bought from the ordinary photo-dealer. It would be beyond the scope of this book to enumerate them all with their special properties. We are mentioning only a few outstanding ones below. Scientists and technologists will be able to obtain further details from the manufacturers of these films. It must be borne in mind that the processing of these materials may radically differ from that of conventional materials. It is therefore essential to study the special processing instructions.

MATERIALS FOR THE GRAPHIC ARTS

A number of special films and plates are on the market for the reproduction techniques of intaglio printers and blockmakers; they are also eminently suitable for other purposes. Some emulsions are very hard and contrasty, others can be stripped so that texts can be mounted on the base. But the smallest quantity available is 25 sheets, so that we must become familiar with the special properties in order to avoid unnecessary expense.

X-RAY SCREEN FILM

This is an ultra-fast orthochromatic emulsion for the photography of X-ray screens. Used for mass radiography in the fight against tuberculosis. Suitable for ordinary use when a fast, non-red-sensitive film is required.

POSITIVE FILMS

These are mainly designed for transparencies but can also be used in ordinary photography. They are particularly suitable for the reproduction of black-and-white originals combining pictures and text. Here, development must be considerably softer than for transparencies. The speed in daylight is about

9 DIN (6 ASA), and in artificial light only about 3 DIN (1.5 ASA). The emulsion is not sensitized, i.e. not colour sensitive. Positive films are available in several formats; they are very cheap in the form of perforated 35 mm film (in bulk).

PHOTOGRAPHIC PLATES

The use of plates is declining more and more. They are now obtainable only for some special purposes. Their main advantage is the perfect planeness of their surface. But they are very fragile and in large quantities their weight is considerable. Plates are sold by the dozen. Black protective paper keeps out the light and prevents fogging. Nevertheless, the box must be opened in the darkroom only, since the pointed glass corners can easily pierce the paper.

For the exposure we insert the plates in darkslides. These must be absolutely free from dust, the cover must move easily, and the felt must be light-tight. To preserve this light-tightness, empty darkslides should be kept with the covers removed, so that the pile of the felt stays erect.

Most darkslides can also be used for sheet film if special adapters are inserted. We must, however, find out by means of a trial exposure whether ground-glass screen- and film plane coincide perfectly. If we photograph the previously-mentioned cm scale at an angle of 45°, any divergency between focusing plane and optimum sharpness will be immediately evident.

TYPES OF PACKING

Photographic films reach the consumer in different types of packing. The most popular is the 35 mm cartridge. Its normal length is 1.65 m (5 ft 5 in) = 36 exposures. 20 exposure-cartridges (length 1 m, 3 ft 4 in) are also available. Since the film is also used for half-frame (18 × 24 mm) and 24 × 24 mm exposures, the numbers along the margin are arranged so that we can clearly identify these formats, too. The latest design of the cartridges requires them to be broken open when the film is to be taken out for development. They can therefore no longer be re-used. This was in any case not advisable since with repeated use the cartridge slit ceased to be light-tight. The film must be wound back into the 35 mm cartridge after the last exposure. Varoius attempts to eliminate rewinding by means of a two-cartridge system have led to success

99

with the rapid cartridge only. But the camera manufacturers have not followed this possibility up with ordinary miniature cameras, because the manufacturers of colour reversal films stipulate that for processing their films be returned in their original cartridges. Some 35 mm films are also available in bulk, normally in 17 m (56 ft) or 30 m (100 ft) length.

Simple and convenient handling has gained the 126 film in cartridges, format 28 × 28 mm, enormous popularity. The film is 35 mm wide, and is supplied only in this special container for 12 or 20 exposures. The cartridge (Kodapak) can be used only in cameras designed for this system.

In the sub-miniature formats the film is also sold in its special container, which is almost invariably designed so that the film need not be rewound.

The most widely used roll film is the 120 type (8 exposures 6 × 9 cm or 12 exposures 6 × 6 cm [$2^{1}/_{4}$ × $2^{1}/_{4}$ in]). For its area it is the most economical photographic material. A certain amount of care is necessary during both the loading and the unloading of the spools to prevent light from entering and fogging the marginal portions of the film.

Sheet films are sold in the formats 6.5 × 9 cm to 18 × 24 cm. Since here the darkslide must be loaded in darkness it is important to know that we are facing the emulsion side when the notch in the film is in the top right hand corner. The standard box contains 25 sheets of black-and-white or 10 sheets of colour film.

The film packs so popular in the early days have been discontinued almost completely. If for some reason or other we require them, we must anticipate long delivery delays and therefore order them in good time.

The fact that ultra-fast films are occasionally more expensive than others means merely that their production is more complicated. They should therefore be used only when the highest speed is essential. For general purposes medium-speed films are preferable.

Filter comparison; summit station, Valluga Railway (Arlberg, Austria).
Top left: without filter. – Top right: with yellow filter. – Bottom left: with orange filter. – Bottom right: with red filter. Photographs by Kisselbach.

The polarizing filter (see p. 107)

Facing page, right: The most important property of this filter, the blocking of polarized light, is best seen if two polarizing filters are slowly rotated relative to each other. The filter in the bottom picture has been turned through 90° from its position in the top picture.

Facing page, left: Similarly it is possible to look through reflecting glass panes if the angle of reflection is suitable for the polarizing filter.

In windscreens made of safety glass, however, the strain areas, too, will become visible.

Leicaflex SL, 90 mm lens, Leitz polarizing filter, filter factor 3.
Photographs by Kisselbach

Right:

In certain directions of the sky the polarizing filter acts like a yellow filter, darkening the blue of the sky and increasing the modelling of the white clouds.

Lech/Arlberg. 50 mm Summicron-R.
Photographs by Kisselbach

*Comparison of
filters
View of
Lake Lugano
from Carona*

*Panchromatic
film*

*Infra-red film
without filter*

*Infra-red film
with infra-red
filter*

Infra-red rays are invisible to the eye. But some films are made that react to them. Since infra-red films are sensitive also to visible light we must use special filters that absorb it. The exposure depends on the infra-red radiation present, the transmission of the infra-red filter and the infra-red film used. The factors are so many that we have to obtain the correct exposures by means of trial series. The manufacturers' instructions will serve as guide lines. Ordinary camera lenses transmit infra-red rays but are not corrected for them. There is a difference in focusing which may be between $1/200$ and $1/400$ of the focal length of the lens used. If we have no time to determine the exact value, we can generally obtain satisfactory results at an extension increase of $1/300$ of the operative focal length and f/11. In terms of a 50 mm lens this means that we have to set the helical focusing mount at 15 m (50 ft) instead of at infinity.

Since our eye cannot see the effect of the infra-red rays, the pictures will often strike us as unusual and surprising. The blue of the sky or of a sheet of water appears almost black; the green of meadows and the foliage of trees is rendered very light, an effect which is caused by the reflection of infra-red by the green leaf pigment, chlorophyll.

Infra-red films must be stored in a cool place. They are grainier than, and their resolving power is inferior to that of, fast black-and-white films. The gradation can be modified by changes in the developing time.

Manufacturer	Film designation	Maximum sensitivity	Limiting sensitivity	Available in
Agfa-Gevaert AG	Scienta 52 A 86	725 to 840 nm	920 nm	30 m (100 ft) rolls
Kodak AG	825 nm	IR 135	875 nm	35 mm 20 exposure cartridge
	810 nm	High Speed Infrared	900 nm	30 m (100 ft) rolls
Orwo	NJ 750	750 nm	825 nm	35 mm cartridge and bulk

FILTERS FOR BLACK-AND-WHITE FILMS

The use of filters has gone very much out of fashion in black-and-white photography. Today mostly yellow, yellow-green, and orange filters are used. Every colour filter has the property of transmitting mainly light of its own colour, lightening it in the picture, whereas it reduces the light of the complementary colour, making it appear darker in the picture.

Yellow filter

This is indispensable in winter sports, because without it shadows in the snow would be deficient in contrast despite sunlight. In the summer it is also very useful in landscape photography. A light blue sky with white clouds, however, does not have its contrast sufficiently increased. The extension factor is $2 \times$.

Yellow-green filter

The effect of this filter resembles that of the yellow filter very closely. In landscape photography it favours the green tones, which is often an advantage. Tanned skin appears a little darker than with the yellow filter. The extension factor for yellow-green filters is $3 \times$.

Orange filter

This is a filter which considerably increases contrast between clouds and the sky, snow and sunlight. It also improves the rendering of distant views, because the yellow and red rays penetrate haze better than light of shorter wave lengths. Portraiture requires great care because the orange filter noticeably lightens the skin tones. Extension factor $3 \times$.

Red filter

Red filters suitable for ordinary panchromatic films are light. They are most useful in high mountain photography, because they strongly cut down atmospheric haze. Cloud effects are enhanced if not dramatized. The extension factor varies a great deal, since the red sensitivity of the film differs between the various brands. We can assume a $6-8 \times$ increase in exposure as a mean value. Red filters are not recommended for films of low red sensitivity.

UV absorbing filter, colourless

This filter has the task of absorbing the disturbing ultra-violet light. It is mostly used in connection with colour film. We can leave it permanently in front of the camera lens as it has no disturbing side effects, but protects it very effectively from sand, salt crystals, and dirt in general. But we must bear the following exceptions in mind: in night pictures containing very powerful light sources, the optically flat filter will reflect these light sources. Although the intensity of the reflected rays is only a fraction of that of the lamp, they will be visible against the very dark shadows of night subjects. Similar disturbances are possible with the sun in the picture. The extension factor of the UV filter is so small that it can be ignored.

Polarizing filter

This is a very interesting filter. Originally its only task was to extinguish reflections from specular surfaces. This effect, however, is limited to certain angle positions and substances, so that polarizing filters are used very rarely. Since sky light, too, is polarized in certain directions, the polarizing filter is much more important in landscape photography. It enables us to differentiate much better between clouds and the blue sky without any colour shift, i. e. to obtain the same effect as with the yellow or orange filter in black-and-white photography.

Neutral-grey polarizing filters are suitable for colour photography. The effect of this filter can be controlled with the eye. It is slowly rotated through 180° in front of it. After the lens is focused the filter is attached to it in the position in which the optimum effect has been found visually. With single-lens-reflex cameras we mount the filter in front of the lens, rotate it, and observe the effect in the viewfinder. The exposure factor is about 3 ×.

LIGHTING AND LIGHT SOURCES

Daylight

The most popular universal light source for photography is the sun. Without doubt the vast majority of pictures are taken in sunlight. The sun changes its position continuously, and not only shines out of a clear blue sky, it often hides behind clouds. This change from brilliant to diffuse lighting also changes the appearance of all the objects surrounding us.

Since we "see" many objects as we remember them, not as they really are, we must develop a keen eye for different illuminations. Only when we observe consciously shall we see that a landscape looks entirely different in the morning from what it looks like at noon, and differs in the glaring light of the summer sun from its appearance in the diffuse light of an autumn day. We must pay particular attention to the direction of the sunlight. It is true that all colours are luminous when we have the sun in the back, but in black-and-white photography this is not such an advantage, because the shadows are absent, and the vivid colours converted into scarcely differentiated grey tones. Contre jour light has a much more three-dimensional effect, although it sometimes produces such contrast as to create other difficulties. With side lighting this risk is generally reduced, especially when reflections are present that soften the contrast. The ideal weather for photography is not, as one might expect, sunlight from a clear blue sky, for it lacks huge, white cumulus clouds, which act as enormous reflectors softening the shadows and reducing the brightness differences to a favourable level.

In architectural photography the light plays a decisive part. There is a certain time of day for many buildings when the sunlight almost glances off the front. This brings stone to life, all ornaments will appear three-dimensional. On a journey we cannot always be on the spot at this ideal time. If we are in a hurry we shall take our picture all the same — as long as we know that we could have made a better job of it in better conditions.

There is no hard and fast rule about what kind of daylight provides the best illumination; this depends much too much on the subject. When the sun is watery, distant views must be ruled out, but there will always be rewarding close-up subjects. Rain, too, can be incredibly attractive, especially in towns and cities; wonderful close-up subjects also abound in rain. Even a foggy day has its photographic appeal. Pictures in the fog, however, are not as simple to take as we might think, because the low contrast increases the exposure latitude of the film. Pictures in fog should be exposed on the short side.

Artificial light

Since we do not always have daylight available, we must very often depend on artificial light sources for our photography. Usually we use halfwatt lamps, although "artificial light" means the whole range from the simple candle to the flash — electronic or bulb. Since the last-named lights up very briefly, it calls for a special exposure technique, and is therefore described in a separate chapter on p. 112.

Special photographic lamps of high light output are on the market in addition to the conventional halfwatt lamps used for lighting purposes; their life, however, is limited, and they are sensitive to shock. If they are used at a lower than their rated voltage life will be considerably extended.

The most modern photographic light sources are the tungsten halogen lamps. Their higher price is justified by their longer life and a light output even higher compared with that of the ordinary photographic lamps.

The various light sources differ not only in their brightness, but also in their colour temperature. This property, however, is of significance in colour photography, where the spectral composition of the light is very important. In black-and-white photography we are interested mainly in intensity. We must remember that fluorescent tubes emit light whose spectrum is not continuous; they are therefore not recommended for colour photography. Whereas in daylight we can as a rule modify the light source only rarely, artificial light offers us many possibilities of adjusting the illumination ourselves. Our eyes tend automatically to balance lighting contrasts slightly, but the film material reacts strictly according to the light intensity. Much experience and practice is therefore necessary for the correct use of artificial light sources.

We must also take into consideration whether our light source emits its light directly, or the light is diffused by gases or a parchment screen, whether reflectors are built in that direct the light to some extent, or condensers bundle it strictly as in a searchlight. We can naturally mix the light from various lamps, but we shall see at the same time how this creates second shadows, although it softens the first ones. One light source should always be dominating. It is a well known fact that the intensity of the light changes in inverse proportion to the change of the square of the lighting distance. In large rooms the reflecting walls are further away than in small ones; this appreciably changes the ratio between direct and reflected light. A brightness difference of 1 : 4 is clearly noticeable even in black-and-white photography.

The very powerful halogen or photoflood lamps have a high current consumption. This does not greatly affect our electricity bill, but we must ensure that the fuses will be strong enough to carry the load. No other appliances of high current consumption (electric radiators etc.) should be switched on at the same time, and when several large lamps are used it is advisable to switch them on one after the other, because the resistance of the cold lamp is lower, and the current surge will be higher during simultaneous switching on.

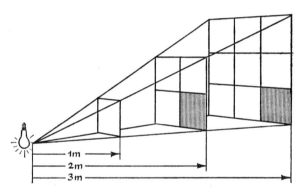

With all artificial-light sources the rule must be observed that the light intensity changes in inverse proportion to the square of the distance.

Lighting with artificial light can be modified to a very great extent. But some experience and practice is required before the correct balance is achieved as a matter of course. It is best to start with a single lamp, and to watch the direction of the shadows carefully. Before we switch the second lamp on we should try to make further use of the light from the first by means of reflecting surfaces such as a projection screen. Where persons are involved, we can often place them so that a bright wall can serve as a reflector. The second

110

Suitable lamps for photography: left: normal version, centre: reflector-type version, right: halogen lamps of still higher light power.

lamp should be less bright than the first, and by varying the lamp distances we can achieve very delicate differentiations. A third lamp may be set up so that its effect is confined to the background.

For professional purposes a spotlight is indispensable, but amateurs can obtain similar effects with a 35 mm projector. The projector lamp must burn in its normal operating position; this means that the projector should not be strongly tilted; the lighting angle required can be obtained with a mirror attached to the projector lens.

If our photographic equipment includes fast lenses such as f/2 or f/2.8, we can take pictures at home in the evening on ultra-fast film in ordinary half-watt lighting. Especially suitable subjects are individuals and small groups when no great depth of field is necessary.

The following table offers information on the lighting performance and the life expectancy of some Osram lamps. Philips supply lamps of similar ratings.

	Volt	Watt	Lumen approx.	Life hrs.	Base
Nitraphot B	220	500	11 000	100	E 27
Nitraphot BR	220	500	3 000*	100	E 27
Halogen 64540	220	650	20 000	15	6 × 6, 35–24
Halogen 64570	220	800	22 000	15	R 7 s–18

* Luminous intensity in the axis of the lamp in candela

111

Flash

Flash, too, is an artificial light source. But since it demands a radically different exposure technique it is treated in a separate chapter. We can see the effect of the other artificial light sources in advance; but the duration of the flash is so short that we cannot judge its lighting effect at all.

There are two distinct types of flash: the flashbulbs, which light up only once, and the electronic flash tubes, which flash again and again. The decision which to buy rests on several factors. If we use flash on rare occasions only, the slightly higher price of the individual flashbulbs will not be a deterrent. We also have the advantage that a much smaller and cheaper unit is required for operating the flash; in addition, the power unit is ready for operation for prolonged periods without special maintenance.

But if we are regular users of flash we shall be better off with an electronic flash unit, although it is considerably more expensive to buy. This is balanced by a negligible running cost per flash, since a single tube is good for many thousands of flashes. Electronic flash units must, however, be regularly used and recharged in order to maintain their performance.

FLASHBULBS

To fire a flashbulb we need a flash unit. The modern versions are very small and accept only capless flashbulbs.

The principle of the flashbulb

Flashbulbs consist of a glass envelope containing a wire mesh of aluminium or zirconium alloy and oxygen under pressure. It is ignited electrically (via an ignition wire or a primer) usually through the discharge of a capacitor charged by a dry battery (15 or 22.5 v). Modern flashbulbs are almost invariably of the capless type, of which there are two versions; this should be borne in mind when flashbulbs are bought. The letter "B" added to the designation of a flashbulb means "blue-tinted". Blue-tinted flashbulbs are now the only ones on the market. They are suitable for both black-and-white and daylight colour film. The tips of flashbulbs have a colour indicator. If it has turned bright pink, the flashbulb will be useless.

The same subject from different camera positions and with lenses of different focal lengths. Poseidon Fountain, Gothenburg, Sweden. Photographs by Kisselbach.

112

Top: Outdoor portraiture is more successful under a slightly overcast sky than in full sunlight. Left, without sunlight; right, in direct sunlight. Both pictures with 90 mm Elmarit-R.

Bottom: The inexpensive expanded polystyrene display dummies are eminently suitable for studying illumination.

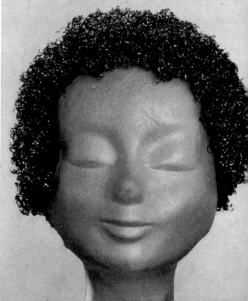

Left: Snapshot on the sportsground with the 280 mm Telyt, very soft sunlight.
Right: Portrait in artificial light, with several lamps.

Bottom: Demonstration of the effect on the facial expression when the angle of incidence of the light is changed.

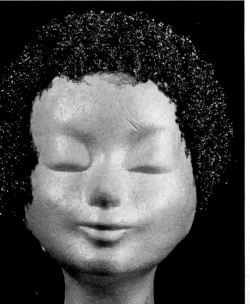

The triangle shows the same grey density on the right and left.

Two identical light sources at identical distances.

Arrangement unchanged, except that the distance of the light source on the right has been doubled. This reduces brightness on the right to one quarter.

The distance of the lamp on the right has been quadrupled compared with that for the top picture. The ratio of illumination is now 1:16. It is no longer suitable for ordinary purposes.

Firing curves

The firing curve below shows the basic differences between X- and M-synchronization. With the X-contact a short flash is fired during a relatively slow shutter speed (usually 1/80 sec); with the M-contact the shutter admits, after pre-ignition, the necessary light quantity from the total output of the flash. Shutter speeds from 1/30 to 1/250 sec depending on the subject.

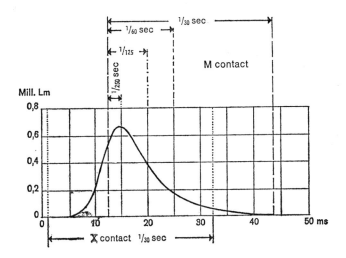

ELECTRONIC FLASH UNITS

Whereas the flashbulb can be ignited only once, the tube of an electronic flash unit can be ignited again and again. It is filled with rare gas which is made to emit an intense flash of light by means of a high-voltage current surge. The flash duration is very short; it lies between 1/500 and 1/2000 sec. Models vary very widely from the small, light-weight amateur unit, of guide number 12, to professional units, weighing many pounds more, of correspondingly higher light power. The performance of the flash unit is dependent on the capacity of the electrolyte condenser to store electrical energy.

Most electronic flash units have a lead or a nickel-cadmium (NC) battery, which supplies them with electrical power. The direct current is converted into alternating current by means of a chopper, stepped up to a high voltage by a transformer, and passed to the capacitor and firing condenser through a rectifier.

117

The following measures are recommended for maintenance: During periods of non-use operate the unit every 3 to 4 weeks until the glowlamp lights up, but do not trigger the flash. After 2–3 months charge the battery, check the acid level, replenish with distilled water if necessary. Even when the unit is used, do not trigger the last flash, but leave the condenser charged. But do switch off the unit itself.

A special version of electronic flash unit employs flash automation. Depending on the type of unit, below a certain flash-object distance the flash intensity is automatically reduced for close-up flash photography. This is done by means of a built-in light sensor, which measures the reflection of the flash actually while it is being fired; when sufficient light has been emitted, the surplus energy is extinguished via a second, special tube built into the flash unit and without light effect.

Here is a practical example: At a distance of 5 m (17 ft) the flash unit operates at full power, flash duration $1/500$ sec. If we reduce the distance to 2.5 m ($8^1/2$ ft) we need not adjust the lens stop or the shutter on the camera; the flash unit exposes only at a quarter of the power, cutting the exposure time to $1/2000$ sec.

Technique of flash exposure

Most commercial flash units are designed for direct connection with the camera. This may be very convenient and also adequate for souvenir pictures, but the frontal light unfortunately produces very flat illumination. The falling-off of light, i. e. the fact that the effect of the light is much more intense in the foreground than in the background, is also very irritating here. Many pictures are instantly recognizable as having been taken with flash.

If we detach the flash from the camera we need a connecting cable. By raising, for instance, the reflector high with our left hand, we obtain much more satisfactory illumination. We must, however, be able to hold the camera and release the shutter with the right hand. If we have a connecting cable of about 1 m (40 in) length, we can use the flashlamp with a certain amount of freedom. Flashing the ceiling is very effective in the average living room, because this produces a completely diffuse reflection and illumination resembling normal room lighting. This "waste of light" means a considerable reduction of the guide number (down to about half), but offers so many advantages in lighting technique that I always recommend it unless there is a risk of underexposure.

In many situations a combination of flash and daylight produces excellent results. We can use it to lighten portions of the subject that are too dark or to deputize for the missing sun. At short distances the flash can be brighter than sunlight. In order to determine the correct shutter speed and lens stop we must begin with the flash intensity. The additional daylight we can determine with the exposure meter. Since with flash photography the shutter speed is often fixed, we must allow for the brightness of the daylight by stopping down the lens. If we use flash outdoors, we shall lose about half a lens stop owing to the absence of reflections from walls. The fact that the intensity of flashlight, too, changes in inverse proportion to the square of the flash distance must also be taken into account.

Limitations of smoke and haze

In very smoky rooms flash pictures will be very flat and devoid of contrast. The flashlight is diffusely reflected as by fog, pictures can be taken only at comparatively short distances.

Electronic flash is a great boon to close-up photography. The manufacturer's guide number is, however, no longer correct within the close-up range. At distances below 1.5 m (5 ft) it must be borne in mind that reflection inside a room has become an almost negligible factor. Hence, special reflectors should be set up or the lens stop opened further.

The guide number is an indication of the intensity of a flash. Its use is based on a simple formula:

$$\frac{\text{Guide number}}{\text{Flash distance}} = \text{Lens stop} \qquad \frac{\text{Guide number}}{\text{Lens stop}} = \text{Flash distance}$$

It represents only an average value for work in normal rooms at medium distances. The guide number is generally given for a speed of 18 DIN — 50 ASA.

The guide number calculation is based on the fact that the intensity of the light varies inversely as the square of the distance of the light and that our

119

aperture scale, too, is designed so that the apertures transmitting the light also change as the square of their diameter.

If we use films of higher speed, we must multiply the guide number for 18 DIN (50 ASA) by the factors in the bottom row:

1	2	3	4	5	6	7	8	9	10	11	12	DIN more
64	80	100	125	160	200	250	320	400	500	640	800	ASA
1.1	1.25	1.4	1.6	1.8	2	2.25	2.5	2.8	3.15	3.55	4	factor

Here is a numerical example. Our guide number for 18 DIN is 30. Our film has a speed of 27 DIN, 9 DIN more. Multiplication factor 2.8 ×. 30 × 2.8 = 84 (new guide number).

The corresponding values are guide number 83 at 50 ASA, and 230 at 400 ASA.

When a film is slower, the guide number decreases by the following factors:

1	2	3	4	5	6	DIN less
40	32	25	20	16	12	ASA
0.9	0.8	0.7	0.6	0.55	0.5	factor

Synchronization means the simultaneous opening of the shutter and firing of the flash. For years all the cameras have had shutters with built-in synchro-contacts.

It must be remembered that there are different types of synchronization. These differences are necessary because flashbulbs suffer from a certain amount of firing delay before they reach their peak intensity. With electronic flash the firing delay is quite negligible. The X-contact normally used here fires after the shutter has been fully opened. A firing delay of 16.5 ms is built into the M-contact. Because of the difference in their function there is also a difference between the feasible speeds of focal-plane and of between-lens shutters. For electronic-flash pictures only those speeds can be used at which the entire film window is exposed simultaneously (mostly 1/50 sec). In between-lens shutter cameras the X-contact is preferred; the shutter speed used, however, is not the shortest, but 1/60 or 1/125 sec is set, because this makes good use of both the full flash intensity and part of the daylight illumination.

The two highlights in the dormouse's eye show clearly that this is a flash picture with two reflectors. The effect of flash is weaker outdoors, because there are no walls to reflect it. 135 mm Hektor, f/11, 1/50 sec. Photograph by Walter Wissenbach.

"Witches Carnival"
at Offenburg, Germany.
50 mm Summicron f/8,
¹/₅₀ sec, electronic flash.

Bowling. f/11, ¹/₅₀ sec,
electronic flash.

Assembly hall, 21 mm
Super-Angulon, ¹/₃₀ sec,
Philips PF 100 flashbulb.

All photographs
by Kisselbach.

Whether the combination of ultra-high-speed film and ultra-fast lenses or flash will be successful can be decided only on the merits of each case.

The examples on the left are typical of the use of flash, sometimes in most difficult conditions at night or in the darkened assembly hall.

The two basketball pictures on the other hand show that sports events today usually do not call for flash any longer. Top: ordinary light, bottom: flash. The top picture has retained of the atmosphere of the game much better.

Photographs: Top by Siegfried Hartig, bottom by Antonio Rudge.

Kittens at play are an enchanting subject to practise on. Since with electronic flash the single flash costs almost nothing, you can flash entire series and forget about the cost. It is better to use a slightly faster film and to stop down a little.

In ordinary rooms, of an average ceiling height of about 2.5 m (8 ft), you can also point your flash at the (white) ceiling. Although this will lose you some of the light, the flashlight character of the lighting will no longer be evident.

Both photographs by Kisselbach.

COLOUR PHOTOGRAPHY

Taking colour photographs is basically very simple. If nevertheless many points that we must consider are mentioned here, this is only to a small extent due to the nature of the colour film as such. The human eye is able to adapt itself also to colours. We see many colours not as they are, but as we remember them. Here is a simple example:

If we approach a house with windows lit by ordinary electric light at dusk on a winter's day we clearly see, contrasting with the bluish snow, that the light of the lamps is yellow-brown. But as soon as we have entered the house, this colour shift has disappeared for us, and we receive a normal impression of all the colours. Our colour film reacts differently and refuses to be deceived. It registers the yellow-brown shift of the artificial light. Our eye, then, is critical only if there is a chance of comparison. The manufacture of colour film is an extremely complicated process, and minor deviations in the film or during processing are unavoidable. But, compared with what our eye overlooks during the exposure, these are very moderate. It is, however, possible to recognize these disturbing factors because they occur according to fixed laws, and to compensate them; in some situations we may abandon the idea of taking the picture altogether because we know in advance that the result will not be satisfactory. Nevertheless, it is a fact that colour photography is easier than its black-and-white counterpart, for every translation of colour values into grey tones is bound to be a compromise. In colour photography we have to consider only the few factors involved in the deception of our eyes.

Additive and subtractive colour mixture

In additive colour mixture "white" is produced by the superimposition of the primary colours red, green, and blue; this, however, can be done only with light rays. Red and green rays superimposed produce yellow.

In subtractive colour mixture "white" is the starting point. The colours (pigments) used subtract light, so that the mixture of the three primary colours involved here — yellow, magenta, cyan — at maximum density produces "black". Essential to subtractive colour photography is the existence of colour separations in the primary colours blue, green, and red.

The colour films on the market today are all based on the subtractive principle. They have three emulsion layers coated on top of one another; the top layer is sensitive to blue, the middle layer to green, the bottom layer to red. During the exposure the appropriate proportions of the colours blue, green, and red are registered in the three layers; these are the colour separations. A strong yellow filter layer prevents the green- and red-sensitive layers from recording blue. The green and red rays must first pass through the top layer, and then through the yellow filter layer; this weakens their energy. The layers for green and red are therefore correspondingly faster. This also explains why colour films are slower than black-and-white ones. Colour reversal and negative films resemble each other in their basic structure. Important differences, however, will be found in their application and processing.

Colour reversal film

The reversal film presents us directly with a colour transparency, which is unique and can be conveniently shown with any projector. Colour quality, resolving power, and richness in tone are unsurpassed. Processing consists of the following stages: the film is first developed black-and-white by means of a special process; black-and-white negatives are produced in all three layers. But no fixation takes place at this stage, and the film is exposed once again to an intense light; this affects the residual silver halides. The hitherto undeveloped silver bromide now forms dyes combined with metallic silver in a colour developer. The following bleach bath converts the metallic silver into a silver salt, which is dissolved out in the fixing bath. What remains in the film is the colour transparency graduated in brightness values.
Colour paper prints can be obtained from colour transparencies. Good results can be expected only when the lighting in the original transparency is balanced, i.e. contrast is not excessive. Failing this we can improve the quality of the print by first making a so-called inter(mediate) neg(ative), and producing the colour prints from this. The costs are considerably higher.

Colour negative film

The exposed colour negative film goes straight into the colour developer, where a negative colour picture is produced in the three layers. Colour paper prints as well as colour transparencies can be obtained from this by means of a similar printing process.

In order to improve the colour reproduction, correcting masks are incorporated in the film, making it appear mainly orange-red, i.e. they mask a large proportion of the colour grades. But this is merely how it appears to the human eye. In reality the colour distinctions have been perfectly preserved. The most modern machinery, developed on the principle of colour television, makes it possible today to see these negatives as positives on a monitor screen and to balance the colour rendering for the subsequent printing. The correction values found are electronically processed. The exposure time is automatically determined with all the corrections allowed for; this results in the optimum quality of the colour print with the predetermined filter values of the colour paper. But since a colour paper print can reproduce only a limited lighting contrast, it is advisable to balance exposure conditions by producing an even illumination that ensures harmonious colour rendering.

COLOUR FILM — TYPES OF PACKAGING

35 mm colour films are supplied almost exclusively in cartridges of 20 or 36 exposures. Longer lengths of film are available for special purposes only (duplicating methods etc.). 126-cartridge films have 12 or 20 exposures.
120 roll film is used for the 6 × 6 ($2^{1}/_{4}$ × $2^{1}/_{4}$ in) format (12 exposures); it is also suitable for the 4.5 × 6 (16 exposures) and 6 × 9 (18 exposures) formats. Larger formats are available only in sheet films.

Daylight colour film and artificial-light colour film

We distinguish between two types of colour reversal material: daylight film, balanced for a colour temperature of 5600° K, and artificial-light colour film, balanced for an average of 3200° K. These different films are necessary because the artificial-light rendering of daylight film differs so radically from our accustomed visual conception that the pictures are totally useless.
Although artificial-light colour film can be adapted to daylight and vice versa by means of suitable filters it is preferable in practice to use the artificial-light film in daylight, because the loss of speed is much less, being almost completely compensated by the higher speed of the artificial-light film. On the other hand, the darker blue filter adapting the daylight film to artificial light reduces the speed by about 6 DIN (75 % of the ASA value).
Blue is the trickiest colour with artificial-light colour film. It shifts more

quickly than the other colours, because the artificial-light emulsion has an inherently excessive blue sensitivity. Compared with daylight, the light from filament lamps is deficient in blue. Warm-tone objects (yellow, red, brown) are therefore less critical in artificial light.

The purchase price of some reversal films includes processing; other films can be processed by the user (recommended only to experts), and commercial processing is not included in the retail price. We can buy the processing vouchers, which we must enclose with the film when we send it to the developing station; this avoids delay in the return of the finished slides.

The finished film may be sent back either in the form of strips or as cardboard- or plastic-mounted slides ready for projection. Glass-less mounting has become increasingly popular, since it has been established that slides are better preserved without than within glass.

Colour negative film is always sold excluding processing costs. Today only one type is available; it is suitable for both daylight and artificial light. Adaptation is carried out during the printing process. When black-and-white prints are to be made of a colour negative, the "universal film" type is recommended; this dispenses with the orange mask, because its colour means an extension of the exposure time for the ordinary black-and-white papers. Special papers for masked films are panchromatic and therefore require different processing methods.

Certain precautions are necessary for the storage of all colour materials. The balance between the three layers will be disturbed if they are stored at too high a temperature. Manufacturers therefore recommend film storage in a cool atmosphere (below 18° C). It is best to place the films in a plastic bag and to keep them in the vegetable compartment of the refrigerator. In these storage conditions the films change very little, so that we can lay in a small stock of the same emulsion batch.

Exposure

Correct exposure plays a decisive role in colour photography. Both in the colour reversal and in the colour negative film the exposure latitude is very narrow. The errors in exposure have, however, different effects. In a reversal film underexposure results in an excessively dense transparency. During first development too little silver had been blackened, leaving too much behind

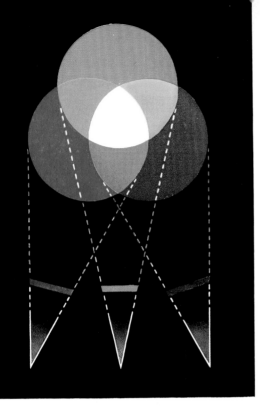

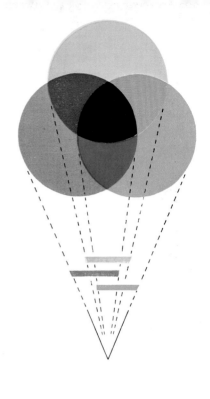

Additive colour mixture   *Subtractive colour mixture*

Blue-sensitive layer — finally yellow
Yellow-filter layer — will be decolorized
Green-sensitive layer — finally magenta
Red-sensitive layer — finally cyan
Anti-halation layer — will be bleached out
Emulsion base

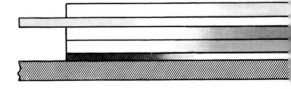

Structure of the colour film for subtractive colour reproduction.

In the colour reversal film first development produces a black-and-white negative, only the second development will convert the residue into a dye image.

In the negative film a complementary-coloured negative is produced directly.

The colour picture is composed of various layers. Of still subjects, you can produce your own colour separation negatives by photographing them on panchromatic film through a suitable blue, green, and red filter in succession. When these black-and-white negatives are printed on colour paper through the corresponding filters, the colour separations will appear in the various colours.

Our modern colour films magically perform this process in a single step simultaneously in three superimposed layers.

However, to be able to judge colour cast, both of illumination and of reproduction, accurately you should be familiar with the basic features of the process.

Top: Yellow separation taken through blue filter.

Middle: Red separation taken through green filter.

Bottom: Blue separation taken through red filter.

Colour negative

Colour negative with mask

Colour positive

The abundance of ultra-violet light at high altitudes often produces a slight blue cast in the pictures. This effect is unpleasant particularly if the foreground is without any saturated colours.

The KR-1.5 filter cuts off both this u.v. portion and a little of the visible blue light. It is specially recommended around midday between 11 and 1 o'clock.

With the KR-3 filter, however, the effect is already too strong.

for the colour development. Overexposure conversely produces too bright a transparency, its highlights are said to be burnt out.

With reversal film we must follow the general rule that the exposure is determined by the pictorially important bright portions. The exposure latitude is slightly influenced by the contrast of the camera subject and may be from half to one aperture step in either direction.

With colour negative film the latitude is a little wider in the direction of overexposure, but narrower towards underexposure. Although slightly underexposed negatives will often still produce good black-and-white prints, there will be a lack of colour in the shadow portions of a colour paper print. Since colour negative films are designed mainly for colour paper prints great care must be taken with the illumination of the subject. Further information will be found in the chapter on Lighting Contrast.

Calibrating the exposure meter

The correct calibration of the exposure meter is very important in view of the narrow exposure latitude of the colour film. It is better to take the test series at half-stop intervals between exposures instead of the whole stop intervals customary in black-and-white photography. The test is carried out as follows:

We determine the exposure for a subject of moderate contrast on a bright day after adjustment of the exposure meter to the speed of our film. The first exposure is taken at a whole aperture stop smaller than measured, the second exposure at half a stop smaller, the third at the measured stop, the fourth at half a stop larger, and the fifth at a whole stop larger. When we receive the film back from the processing station, the results will show us whether our exposure meter and our camera outfit are well matched or we have to correct by half or even a whole stop. The additional refinements of exposure measurement as described on p. 62 in the chapter on black-and-white technique mostly apply also to colour photography. Reversal films can accommodate a considerably greater subject contrast than colour negative films.

Measuring the lighting contrast

If we want to measure the lighting contrast for colour negative film, we can use the exposure meter:

133

We take a reading of a sheet of white paper first held at the brightest spot of the subject; this is followed by a reading of the paper held at the darkest spot required still to appear in colour in the print. The difference between the two pointer deflections represents the lighting contrast; it should not exceed two stop values.

Schwarzschild Exponent

In very poor lighting conditions colour films show a certain loss in sensitivity. For daylight film the full sensitivity is determined for shutter speeds of $1/60$ and $1/125$ sec. If this film is used inside a church where the exposure time measured increases to 1 sec, it must be further increased to 2 sec to avoid underexposure.

Artificial-light films are calibrated for a shutter speed of about $1/2$ sec. A noticeable speed loss will be evident only at 8 sec exposure time and longer. The fact that a loss in film speed occurs at low lighting intensities was first discovered by the astronomer Schwarzschild, and is therefore called the Schwarzschild Exponent. Since our three emulsion layers have different speeds, a colour shift occurs in addition. As this varies with the make of colour film it is advisable to obtain further information from the film manufacturer if there is frequent occasion to use long time exposures.

Colour temperature

This is a term loaned from physics. It can easily lead to wrong ideas in the layman, because in everyday usage we describe blue and green as cold, yellow and red as warm colours. The concept of colour temperature is based on the phenomenon that the colour of the light a glowing body emits changes as the temperature of the body rises or falls. When a piece of iron is only at red heat, its temperature will be lower than when it is at white heat. The same applies to light sources. The whiter their light the higher their colour temperature, the greater their spectral proportion of blue.

Our most important light source is the daylight. In sunlight its colour temperature is in the neighbourhood of 5600° K. °K (Kelvin) is the measuring unit of colour temperature. It begins at Absolute Zero (−273° C), i.e. it differs by this value from the centigrade scale. But since we do not photograph with sunlight alone and also use a large proportion of the scattered light from the sky, the latter's colour temperature, too, plays a part. The blue sky light alone corresponds to a radiation from 7000 to 27000° K. This makes it only too obvious that blue cast is unavoidable if we use this sky light exclusively, i. e. in the shadow cast by the sun.

To perceive differences in daylight illumination visually requires some practice. Our eye estimates most efficiently if it has comparison values to guide it. A sheet of white paper in the sun compared with a white surface in the shade clearly reveals the blue cast of the latter. How strongly the sunlight is affected by our atmosphere becomes apparent during sunset, when the colour temperature drops to 2300° K; at such a great difference everybody will see it clearly. But the small changes in the blue proportion are not seen at first; the reason for this is the change in the atmosphere. During sunset the light reaches the earth at a very oblique angle; the short-wave blue light is much more strongly deflected than the long-wave red light.

When precise values are required, the colour temperature must be determined with a specially designed measuring instrument, which has two photo-electric cells, of which one is blue-, the other red sensitive. At 5600° K the pointer is at zero; when the light becomes more red, the pointer will drift towards the red, when it becomes more blue, towards the blue sector of the scale. The instrument is accompanied by detailed operating instructions. Essential to the perfect functioning of the colour temperature meter is a certain minimum intensity of the light. Another essential requirement is that the light source emits a continuous spectrum.

The following list provides a survey of the colour temperature of various light sources:

DAYLIGHT, in °Kelvin, mean values
direct sunlight, a. m. and p. m., sky with white clouds	5600
sunny, clear blue sky	6000—6600
completely overcast high grey sky	7000—12000
blue sky without direct sunlight (i. e. in the shade)	7000—27000
setting sun	2300

candlelight	1800
40 W filament lamp	2600
200 W filament lamp	2800
type B photoflood (new)	3200
type S photoflood (new) and halogen lamp	3400
blue-tinted flashbulb	about 6000
electronic flash	5600—7000

Fluorescent tubes do not emit a continuous spectrum. We therefore cannot determine any colour temperature. The quality of the light lies between day- and artificial light. If we use fluorescent tubes mixed with other light sources, the results will be satisfactory. The warmer types should be combined with type B photofloods, and artificial-light colour film used. The intensity of the photofloods should be twice to three times that of the fluorescent tubes.

Mixed light

We frequently find ourselves in situations in which there is a mixture of day- light and artificial light. Theoretically no balance is possible. In practice, however, interesting effects will be produced, especially on artificial-light film. The daylight proportion must not be dominant, its effect should be restricted to a blue cast in a few areas. The intensity ratio should be such that in the correctly exposed artificial-light portions the light from the fila- ment lamps is about four times stronger than the daylight.

On daylight film, areas illuminated by light from filament lamps is rendered yellow-brown. If the daylight is insufficient for interior subjects, we can supplement it by means of electronic flash or blue-tinted flashbulbs of the same colour temperature. Additional filament lamps will not be disturbing provided the intensity of the daylight is 2—3 times stronger.

Facing page: "Fast Filippo" at Naples. Rolleiflex, Xenotar, f/16, ¹/₂ sec, Agfacolor CN 17. The camera followed the subject; intentional unsharpness in order to obtain this picturesque effect. Photograph by Thorsten Rehbinder.
pp. 138/139: The Grand Canyon, Arizona, is a grandiose spectacle of nature. The late afternoon sun conjures up a magic depth. Rolleiflex, Planar, f/5.6, ¹/₆₀ sec. Ektachrome X, 19 DIN, 64 ASA. Photograph by A. Baege.

Filters for colour photography

In colour photography the use of filters is based on conditions entirely different to those in black-and-white work. With few exceptions (U.V. absorbing-, polarizing filters) filters for black-and-white are unsuitable for colour film. We distinguish between two types of filter, differing in their use.

CONVERSION FILTERS

Conversion filters adapt colour films to use in a type of light for which they were not designed. Their dye is correspondingly strong. The method of using artificial-light film in daylight has been found really reliable in practice. Conversion filters suitable for this purpose are Kodak No. 85 B and KR 12. The first is a gelatine filter, the second is dyed in the mass. The results of their conversions are very good, whereas the other method, i. e. the use of daylight colour film in halfwatt light with the Kodak 80 B gelatine filter or KB 12 dyed-in-the-mass filter is less recommended because this involves a 6 DIN (75 % ASA) loss of speed.

We can raise the colour temperature of the light with a weak blue filter, e. g. when we want to use ordinary halfwatt lamps with artificial-light colour film balanced for 3200 °K.

CORRECTION FILTERS

form another group. They are finely graduated filters with which we are able to correct slight variations in the illumination. The use of these filters requires sufficient experience and knowledge of the direction in which the colour rendering has to be corrected.

In actual practice only the professional photographer will find complete correction necessary. For the amateur it is enough to subdue any excess in

Top: Laser beam passing through a sheet of ruby of 0.5 mm thickness in about ¹/₁₀₀₀ sec. Magnification 8 ✕. Rolleiflex SL 66, 150 mm Sonnar, f/8, open shutter.
Below: Thin polished section of granite between crossed Nicol filters. The crystalline composition of a rock sample can be made visible and analysed through the interference colours it produces between two polarizing filters when they are rotated. Rolleiflex SL 66 (without lens), and polarizing microscope. 2.5 ✕ objective, 10 ✕ eyepiece. Agfacolor CK 20. Both photographs by Andreas Pahlitzsch.

the illumination because the eye completes the correction during projection. For photography in daylight two weak pink filters are therefore adequate.

The KR 1.5 is the most important filter. It pushes the colour rendering a little towards "warmer" and is useful whenever an appreciable proportion of U.V. light is present, e.g. with distant views under a deep blue sky etc. — The colour temperature of quite a number of electronic flash units is so high that here, too, KR 1.5 makes the colour rendering more pleasing. The effect can be readily demonstrated with a few comparison pictures with and without filter.

The test pictures should include a piece of grey cardboard or a step wedge. They provide a good indication whether the colour rendering is neutral.

We must not use this filter if we do not want to reduce the blue content of the light, for instance when the sun is low.

The effect of the KR 3 filter is considerably stronger. It is used only very rarely, when the blue proportion is so dominant that a KR 1.5 would be too weak. Such exceptions are pictures in the shade under a deep blue sky and certain underwater pictures. Comparison pictures including a piece of grey cardboard in normal light show at once that the colour has been shifted towards brownish.

For the professional photographer a very large assortment of finely graduated gelatine filters in green, red and blue as well as in the complementaries yellow, cyan, and magenta is available in a range of different densities. The use of these filters is essential in advertising photography where certain colour hues must be reproduced as accurately as possible.

THE POLARIZING FILTER

Polarizing filters, which are practically neutral grey, are also suitable for colour photography. In addition to their polarizing effect they have the property of cutting off all the U.V. light. Since the sky light is partially polarized, it offers an effective field for the use of this filter. With a suitable filter position clouds in a blue sky gain in contrast because the blue sky will be rendered darker. Haze in distant views will be cut down. All the other well-known effects such as the extinction or reduction of non-metallic reflections, specular reflections from pictures or sheets of water, can be produced as in black-and-white photography.

With single-lens-reflex cameras we mount the filter in front of the lens and slowly rotate it until we see the desired effect. The camera angle decides the effectiveness of the filter. After a rotation of the filter through 180°, its effect will be identical.

If we cannot observe the effect of the filter mounted directly on the camera lens, we rotate it in front of the eye until it produces the desired effect, and transfer it to the lens in this position.
The extension factor of polarizing filters is about 3 $\times$.

Flash

Since we prefer to use daylight film in our camera, it is desirable to have light sources which have daylight characteristics to supplement the sunlight. This applies to the small flashbulbs, now available only blue-tinted, and to electronic flash units, whose colour temperature is matched to daylight and therefore allows us to replace the missing sun in dull weather outdoors, or to intensify the sunlight for close-up subjects. We can lighten the foreground in contre jour light and soften excessive lighting contrast with these sources. The most important technical information about work with flash has already been provided in the chapter on flash photography. An additional point must be considered in colour photography: any falling-off in brightness leading to underexposure will also produce a colour shift. One of the most important data in flash photography is the intensity of the flash and, when daylight and flash is combined, the correct balance between the two intensities. The guide number (p. 119) is a valuable yardstick. In the very popular method using the flash directly on the camera we have a frontal illumination which delivers the correct brightness practically only in a single plane. Anything in front of it will be over-, anything behind it underexposed. If we have a chance to arrange the flash a little above the camera, and if in addition bright walls improve the reflection, the illumination will at once be more balanced; colour rendering, too, will be improved. Those very keen on close-up photography will find the great intensity of the flash in the near-focusing range indispensable. But the guide number given by the manufacturer no longer applies, and we must obtain information about the effective performance of our flash unit by means of our own experiments. The method of using 50 cm (20 in) as reference distance has been found reliable. Light cardboard reflectors must be set up around the object to be photographed so that the shadows will be sufficiently softened. Exposure factors caused by the additional extension required by close-up subjects must also be remembered. Since we cannot influence the effect of the flash at will by opening and closing the lens diaphragm, we must make the adjustment by varying the flash distance. For instance, at a distance of 35 cm (14 in) the illumination from a flash is twice as bright as at a distance of 50 cm (20 in).

Tips for colour photography

> Sunshine with reflecting clouds is ideal.
> In hazy sunlight close-up subjects are preferable.
> Watch the lighting contrast, soften shadows that are too heavy. Frontal lighting (sun in the back) produces luminous colours, side lighting strong modelling. Extreme contre jour light demands great care, especially in front of dark subjects. Contre-jour light subdues the colours.
> Close in on your subject. Subject trimming is not possible with colour reversal film.
> Distant views with foreground have a better effect of depth, but they are rewarding only when the air is very clear.
> Colours should be used sparingly. Avoid a hotchpotch.
> Subjects of almost no colour often make very attractive pictures in colour.
> Choose quiet backgrounds.
> Distinguish between fore- and background colours.
> Warm colours (yellow and red) have a better effect in the foreground, cold ones (blue and green) in the background. In practice, of course, this is not always realizable.

Opposite: These delicate flowers obtain their effect from the colour patches in the background.
Leica, 135 mm Hektor, f/5.6, 1/100 sec, Agfacolor CT 18. Photograph by Hermann Roth.
p. 146: Negro boy in Amboseli Park. For portraits of this kind harsh sunlight must be avoided. Open eyes and a relaxed facial expression can be expected in soft light only. Leicaflex, 90 mm Elmarit-R, 1/125 sec, Ektachrome X film.
p. 147: Giraffes in Amboseli Park. The slight haze softens the usually harsh illumination. 280 mm Telyt, f/5.6, 1/250 sec. Both photographs by Julius Behnke.

Marabu, Kenya. Leica M 2, 200 mm Telyt, f/4, $^1/_{60}$ sec, Kodachrome II. From the Leica Colour Slide Competition. Photograph by Michael von Rosen.

148

> Watch out for coloured reflections (persons under trees, sunshades).
> Choose as high a shutter speed as possible. It is better to have less depth of field and no camera shake. Standard exposure time 1/125 sec.
> Choose as shallow a depth of field as possible. Blurred background often enhances the modelling of colour subjects.
> Rain offers interesting motifs in large cities.
> Night shots are most successful in twilight. Choose short enough exposures to obtain the night effect, and to avoid flare around the light sources in the picture.
> If possible, avoid the use of filters for night pictures; their plane-parallel surfaces reflect the light sources.
> Load and unload your camera in the shade.
> Colour films should be processed as soon after exposure as possible, particularly in hot climates.
> Portraits are most successful in very soft illumination, because when the light is too harsh and bright the sitters tend to squint. Bounce flash at the ceiling is not recommended if the ceiling is coloured.
> Photoflood lamps change their colour temperature with age.
> Photography with a single lamp is difficult because the rapid falling off of the light towards the background results in colour shift.
> Lighting for colour photography should be softer and more balanced than for black-and-white.
> During sunset, the colour temperature of the sun will have dropped below 3000° K. On artificial-light emulsion sunsets will be reproduced more reddish than yellowish-brown, which appears more neutral.
> Daylight film can also be adapted by means of the blue conversion filter KB 9 or KB 12. This causes a loss in film speed of 4 and 6 DIN (60 and 75 % of the ASA value) respectively.
> Ordinary exposure measurement does not produce reliable results during sunsets.

These rules should serve the beginner as signposts and save him disappointment. The advanced worker knows that we cannot force photography into a straightjacket and that often the very attraction of a colour picture is based on an offence against the rules.

PROJECTION

Projection is the most impressive method of showing photographs. All the delicate tone gradations can be reproduced without loss in the transparency which, because it is transilluminated, can record a much longer brightness range than a paper print. For the three-dimensional effect of a picture its dimensions are of decisive importance. Our eyes perceive a picture as more realistic when it is larger. A certain relationship exists between the effective picture area and the viewing distance. Since we cannot normally afford the expense of large enough prints (the question of space also arises) the simpler and indeed superior way of viewing is slide projection.

Prints in the 7×10 cm ($^1/_4$ pl.) format for the photo album can be viewed by only 2–3 persons at a time. A slide show, on the other hand, will always be a group experience.

What is shown and how it is shown is a question of great importance. The effect is based not on the quantity, but on the quality of pictures, on a well-balanced selection. A show before a large audience should be well prepared.

The commentary should be composed like an entertaining story. It is of course much easier to give a talk accompanying a slide show, because picture follows picture, and we can take our cue from what appears on the screen. The normal duration of such a show is an hour, and hour and a half with special subjects. Anything longer than this will tire the audience. The more pictures we show the less time will there be for a commentary for each. But we must not talk without let-up, some pictures need silence to make an impact.

80 to 100 slides are quite enough for a lecture. It matters little whether we use a semi- or a fully automatic magazine projector; the magazine always offers the advantage of the slides being immediately ready for projection once they have been placed in the correct order. They also remain free from fingermarks, since they are not touched by hand during projection. Do not leave the magazines standing in the open where they merely collect dust.

150

Hints for perfect projection

The projection screen has a great influence on the quality of projection. A sheet with creases must be regarded as a most makeshift solution; stout drawing paper off a roll is much to be preferred. Because of their special impregnation and pure white colour projection screens have a high reflecting power and do not attract dirt as readily as ordinary linen. Recently, washable plastic screens of very good reflecting power have become available. In view of the high light output of the projectors, the use of metallized screens has become unnecessary; they suffer from the disadvantage that the image brightness depends very much on the viewing angle.

It is best to *set up the projector* behind the viewers in order to eliminate disturbance owing to stray light. The table shows the focal length required at a given projection distance and screen image size. The maximum viewing distance from a screen image should, if possible, not be longer than 6 times the width of the image. The viewers in the front row, too, should be sufficiently far away from the screen (about $1^1/_2 \times$ the image width). The screen should be fixed high enough so that the slides can be projected above the viewers' heads. Projection should be at right angles to the screen. If the projector has to be tilted the screen, too, should, if possible, be tilted. A firm support for the projector is also important.

The mains cable should be arranged so that the projector is not accidentally pulled off its support. Never move the projector when it is switched on: if the coils of the filament touch each other because of the resultant vibration, the lamp will be overloaded and burn through. Before switching on the lamp make sure that the mains voltage is correct. Projector lamps have only a limited life. For important slide lectures a spare lamp should always be at hand.

Projection will be really luminous only if the room is completely blacked out. Stray light is very disturbing. If for some reason projection is required in a semi-darkened room, a particularly powerful instrument must be used and the size of the image must be much smaller.

151

PHOTOGRAPHY IN PRACTICE

Family chronicle

It would be the right thing to begin a family chronicle with pictures of the wedding. But difficulties are bound to arise at your own wedding. Here, selftimers are of only limited assistance. Very often we can give the happy couple a really personal present by recording the course of events in a series of pictures. The most difficult photographs to take are those of the wedding ceremony in church. The vicar will be in charge of the proceedings and it is a matter of tact to ask his permission first. This will mostly be granted, especially if we promise not to use flash and act with the required restraint during the solemn rite.

In order to be able to do without flash we need to use ultra-fast black-and-white film, as well as a fast f/2 or f/1.4 lens. In churches with bright windows it is very often possible to obtain good colour pictures. When we work without flash we have the great advantage that the genuine atmosphere is preserved.

Some of the most impressive views will be the return of the bride and groom to the entrance of the church with the nave as background (depending on lighting conditions). If the church is very dark or the technical equipment inadequate there remains the obligatory picture in front of the church. If steps lead up to the door, we can make a good group picture here. A large gathering can be photographed to advantage only if steps or similar supports are available on which to arrange the many members of the group. If there are any curious onlookers about, one or two snapshots of them will be a welcome addition to the wedding album.

Unfortunately many beautiful wedding customs are becoming increasingly rare. But when the celebrations take place in the home or in a restaurant etc. many merry scenes worthy of a snapshot will occur at a late hour. Here, too, we need ultra-fast film and lenses if we want to make do without flash. In a very smoky atmosphere flash should be used with care, as the murkiness will make the pictures look flat. When inserting a film before a wedding we must make doubly sure that the film transport mechanism functions correctly.

In addition to the usual "posed" pictures we should always attempt a snapshot too. f/5.6, $^1/_{250}$ sec.

Left:
Modern churches present no problem to the photographer who wants to take his pictures hand-held on ultra-high-speed film at f/2 without flash. If the noise of the camera shutter is disturbing, it can be "synchronized" with the organ music.

Right:
You must be generous with film during a wedding reception in a hotel or at home. Here, too, flash tends to destroy the atmosphere. Do not forget to make doubly sure of correct film transport when you load your camera.

Photographs of christenings and communions or confirmations do not differ a great deal from a technical angle. If you have little experience you can familiarize yourself with your subject by first taking photographs in similar lighting conditions.

The children's growing up, birthdays, first day at school, visits to the grandparents etc., the whole family chronicle are an important chapter of photography, because they create goodwill towards our hobby among our better halves.

Pictures of our home town or village, our flat or house are also part of this chronicle, and we shall be glad later on that we also took pictures from everyday life.

Touring, holidays, landscapes

A journey will be the more interesting the better we prepare for it. Even then, impressions will be so plentiful that our memory can absorb only a very modest part of them. If we have been able to supplement our impressions with photographs, we can in the peace and quiet of our home relive and gain a deeper insight into many events. We shall be surprised how many interesting details we shall discover in our pictures that had completely escaped us at the time simply because there was too much to see.

A camera with several lenses of different focal lengths offers its owners the extraordinary advantage that they can take both general views and important detail from one and the same camera position.

For interesting street scenes we must use a special snapshot technique. The camera should therefore be prepared by pre-selected shutter speed and lens stop settings so that all we have to do before we press the button is to make a slight last-second correction of the focusing. When we take street scenes prolonged fumbling with our camera will attract attention: we therefore focus in a different direction on an object at about the same distance as our real object, swivel the camera round at the right moment and release the shutter. When we have distances for comparison, our estimates will be quite reliable.

This typical wide-angle shot in slight contre jour light is sharp from the near foreground to the depth of the subject, owing to a small lens stop.

With a 35 mm lens in our 35 mm camera we can use a method based on the following consideration: the object distance corresponds to the width of the picture, because the negative width of 36 mm is almost the same as the lens focal length of 35 mm. It is relatively easy to aim the lens at the centre of the picture and to estimate the distance along the ground with the eye. With this method the camera remains in the ever-ready case or on the chest suspended from the neck strap, and we press the button without raising our camera to the eye. After only a few trial films we shall have effective control of the picture area we wish to cover, and shall be surprised how well we are able to aim with the lens, and how few people notice that we are taking a photograph when we do not raise our camera to our eye.

In order to obtain colour photographs of a uniform colour rendering during a trip we must buy films of the same emulsion batch number; before setting out on the journey, we expose a trial film so that we become thoroughly familiar with its characteristics.

We should always insert our own films. We cannot expect anyone else to take the same amount of care. The camera models are so many, and a stranger may easily miss the finer points of handling an individual camera. Breakdowns of the film transport are by no means rare after incorrect insertion.

During travel in hot countries for prolonged periods we should take an ice box or at least an expanded-polystyrene container along to protect our stock of films from the effects of temperatures above 30 °C. Under the southern sun temperatures in the glove compartment of the parked car reach 40 °C and even 50 °C. Remember the last bar of gooey chocolate you found in it?

Exposed colour films should be developed as soon as possible. Unfortunately, dispatch to the processing laboratory back home is sometimes subject to formalities. If the journey does not take longer than 4 weeks, it is best to take all the exposed films back in the personal luggage and to have them developed together. If, however, reliable processing stations exist in the country of our visit, it is very convenient to be able to see the first results which if good will encourage us. Faulty results, too, will give valuable hints; we might even be able to repeat one or the other unsuccessful picture.

To take notes en route is warmly recommended, but very rarely done. In black-and-white photography where the price of the negative material does not matter a great deal the following method has been found reliable. We write important hints and data on a sheet of notepaper with a felt-tipped pen, and photograph the notes for future information on the negatives. This method has been found particularly useful if pictures are to be sent elsewhere for titling (editors). In such cases we should do the same with colour pictures. There are some sound reasons why we are dealing with the subject of land-scapes separately. If a landscape fascinates us, it does not follow that it is necessarily photogenic. We usually try to capture the grandiose features of a landscape with a wide-angle lens. Often we should do the opposite, use a longer focal length and pick out only a few, but typical, elements. This concentration and simplification and at the same time preservation of the atmosphere is the great and difficult task of landscape photography.

Often the atmosphere is delicate; much more so than we suspect, in the transitions because here, too, our eye is influenced by the colours. It will therefore be a good idea to place a few strong accents in the foreground so that the impression of softness does not predominate. With black-and-white film a yellow filter will be particularly useful in strong sunlight with a blue sky, because it prevents the blue from appearing too pale. Sometimes we can dramatize our subject by using an orange filter. When in doubt, we take the subject through several filters and select the atmosphere most suitable for it at home.

Snow and ice

Photography in the snow should really be quite easy. Brightness is ample, and the black-and-white gradation is automatically provided by the snow. Nevertheless a few points are worth considering. Even when the sun is shining the snow has too little contrast for our black-and-white films. A yellow filter puts this right, an orange filter exaggerates it slightly.

Side lighting is good, contre jour lighting better. Owing to the reflections from all sides contre jour lighting is never as contrasty here as in ordinary conditions.

Lines and shapes are of special importance; so are interesting close-ups. Fast-moving skiers can be shown well only with long-focal-length lenses. A particularly exciting view is that from the opposite slope.

Wrong exposures are more frequent with winter subjects than we expect. The causes are firstly the very great brightness, and secondly the completely different brightness distribution compared with that of the standard object, on which the calibration of our exposure meters is based. When the snow constitutes more than 70 % of the whole subject, exposure must be twice that indicated by the meter. In contre jour light it will sometimes be useful to take a shadow reading of the snow and use this for the exposure.

Only rarely will snow and ice be photogenic without sun. This applies equally to pictures in colour.

With colour film we must use a KR-1.5 filter at high altitudes in order to reduce the large blue and U.V. proportion of the light there (except within 2 hours of sunrise and sunset — otherwise the snow will be tinged with red).

Ice ferns on the window are interesting close-up subjects. We point, if possible, the camera so that we have a dark area behind the window. The close-up reading in this direction yields the correct value. Icicles should be treated similarly. Contre jour light and a dark background are favourable.

All kinds of ice sport demand instant readiness for action and complete mastery of the camera controls, because here movements are very fast indeed. Events in artificial light (ice hockey matches, ice revues) create the additional difficulty of requiring ultra-fast films and large apertures. Here, the only way out is to focus at a suitable distance and to wait until something interesting happens in the focusing plane. A further tip for ice revues: we watch the performance first to familiarize ourselves with it, and earmark the most impressive scenes. Since everything is repeated with great precision, we shall be well prepared for our photographic adventure.

Reportage

We are living in the age of mammoth illustrated weeklies and colour supplements. We all have looked at a picture reportage of an interesting event, and although we see only a few pictures we have the feeling as if we were there in person. A complicated, prolonged action has been captured in a few pictures. Naturally, those actually published are mostly only an extract from what had been photographed; but the selection only compresses the action, provided the main phases have been recorded.

This brings us to the most important element: photographic reportage is first and foremost an intellectual exercise. What little it requires of photographic technique merely creates the foundation. Naturally, all good reporters are superb masters of their cameras, and have many accessories from the wide-angle to the telephoto lens so that they can adapt themselves to difficult

Dog team with sledge in a snowstorm in Lapland. This picture is most remarkable in that the photographer considered neither himself nor his camera in order to operate in this fearful snowstorm. The yellow filter has produced fine differentiation of the texture of the snow. f/5.6, ¹/₅₀₀ sec, photograph by Leif Geiges.

p. 162: Here, too, the yellow filter conjures detail in the snow. 280 mm Telyt, photograph from the opposite slope, direct contre-jour light, yellow filter. Photograph by Prof. Hoppichler.

p. 163: Parachutist. The photograph was taken immediately after the jump. 50 mm Summicron, f/5.6, ¹/₁₀₀₀ sec, photograph by Maurice Lamaud.

In such situations the action-readiness of the 35 mm camera is a great advantage.

situations. But it is the reporter's mental faculty that has to decide: what is happening here, where is the best viewpoint, when will the climax be, how will it continue?

Almost all of us have witnessed situations in which a picture report would have been most impressive. We should therefore always take enough exposure material with us to have a reserve for such contingencies.

Here, too, the well-tried rule applies: we must practise, try to make something even of many opportunities that do not appear very important, in order to master the technique when we are faced with a really challenging task. In this field we must make a clear distinction between the reportage, which tells a story in pictures, and the picture series, which consists of pictures of the same nature, that need not, however, be related in time. Usually the series is much simpler, and offers opportunities for practice, for training our mental faculties a little. There is no strict dividing line between reportages and picture series; both are worth cultivating because they improve both our technical and our mental abilities.

Movement- and sports photography

Good movement- and sports photographs are among the technical top achievements. Here it is really necessary to have all the aspects of camera operation at one's fingertips, all manipulations must be second nature; there must also be a certain instinct for what is going to happen next, because of the few hundredths of a second's delay before we press the button. We can preset lens stop and shutter speed, but when we use long-focal-length lenses, focusing must often wait until the last moment. In some situations we can let the moving subjects enter the focusing plane, but even this requires much practice and experience.

Let us begin with movement shots. First question: What phase of the movement is favourable, i.e. when is the right moment? We have already recommended elsewhere in this book to take the first steps in this direction with "persons walking". If we want our subjects to be frame-filling, this will not

Such rapid sequence shots with long-focal-length lenses can be obtained only with a motor. This offers the ski instructor valuable information about the course of the pupil's movement. Leicaflex SL mot, 400 mm Telyt, f/8—11. Photographs by Prof. St. Kruckenhauser.

be as easy as one might think. At the next step we must practise exactly like the dancing couple we want to photograph. We should know the typical phases of a dance intimately. The camera position, too, must be considered, so that the figures will make an impact. It may become necessary for us to kneel in order to improve the camera angle and the perspective.

Unfortunately there are no hard and fast rules, but the more we know about the subject, the more familiar we are with the sport concerned, the better we shall be able to capture the typical moment. But we must be as quick operationally as we are mentally.

The question of film consumption must never enter into the picture. To expose one, two films within a short period of time is no waste. Economy will become important only when we inspect our negatives in the enlarger, and decide on what is really worth enlarging. When taking practice shots we can project them as negatives in our 35 mm projector; all technical qualities and shortcomings will be clearly revealed at 1×1.5 m (40×60 in) on the projection screen.

A particular point to practise in sports photography is coordination of subject distance and optimum format utilization in the viewfinder.

Here is an example: Imagine a gate in a slalom race; each competitor has not only to pass it, he also has to turn here. But we must keep a distance of more than 10 m (33 ft) for safety reasons. The shortest focal length for the 35 mm format is therefore 135 mm. Often an even longer focal length is required to make the subject fill the negative. To press the button, at just the right moment, with such long focal lengths after hours of waiting in cold and wind calls for patience, experience, and competence. Only after we have tried our hands at such subjects ourselves can we appreciate the effort that must have gone into many a sports picture.

Sports scenes involving rapid movement require high shutter speeds. At $1/500$ or $1/1000$ sec we must open the lens stop very wide, which leaves us with very little depth of field. We shall often go to the threshold of underexposure rather than take a picture of insufficient sharpness. It is a well-known fact that we can increase the effective speed of a film by forced development. Both an extension of the developing time at the standard temperature and an increase in the temperature of the developer at the standard developing time are possible. This forced development, however, unpleasantly increases the contrast of the negative in the normally exposed portions. All pictures should therefore receive short exposures. But the method is risky without preliminary trials with the same emulsion batch and an accurate exposure meter. The usual gain in speed is in the region of 2, sometimes even 3 lens stops. It can make an enormous difference to the result whether we can use f/4 or f/8 for a subject.

Grandad in front of the camera

Of all fields of photography, the human element is often the most valuable to us. Most people initially display a certain self-consciousness in front of the camera. Nor do they like to go to a photographer and it is by no means rare that as soon as a person has died one is horrified to realize that no decent picture exists of the departed

It is not as if the conditions for obtaining satisfactory portraits in a room with a few large windows were not very good indeed. But we do not want to copy the studio of a professional photographer; we set up instead either our projection screen, if it measures at least 1.25 $\times$ 1.25 m (4 $\times$ 4 ft), or a sheet of drawing paper measuring 1.5 $\times$ 1.5 m (5 $\times$ 5 ft) parallel to and about 1.5 m (5 ft) away from our window. Even a white table cloth might do. This creates a narrow passage, a little space near the window, considerably lighter than the rest of the room and at the same time favourably illuminated by this reflecting screen. The light is bright enough to enable us almost always to use instantaneous shutter speeds at f/4 with a 35 mm camera. But we are taking our photograph parallel to the window. Since everything is a matter of practice, we place a very patient person on a stool as our first "guinea pig", at about the last third of the row of windows. The stool is important, because when we sit on a chair, we usually lean against it; this narrows the angle between chin and throat, and the latter will appear thicker than necessary. On the stool our model sits at a half turn, but with a slight shift of the weight towards the front; to sit a little more comfortably, he or she props the arm on the knee.

This posture tends to tighten the skin along the throat, so that creases disappear. A further advantage is that the model can be very conveniently observed. Since the light comes from one side, the eyes are not affected by the strong light, and are therefore wide open. With spectacle wearers the chances of reflections are reduced, and it is easier than outdoors to cut them down further by slight turns of the head.

Often it would be best to take about 10 "exposures" without transporting the film. This will relax our sitter considerably. Now we can suggest slow turns of the head to the left and to the right in order to record the most favourable aspect of the sitter's face. In the past, German regulations for passport photographs demanded a half profile, with the left ear visible. A clear example of this posture will be found on German banknotes, all of which bear a reproduction of a portrait by some Old Master. At the same time this shows us the favourable position of the shadow lines and how it prevents the face from appearing too broad. Nor should the background be ignored; it should not be too close, and as restful as possible.

Children

Children's pictures are the Amateur Subject Number One. One might even be tempted to say: show me your children's pictures, and I shall tell you how good a photographer you are. Basically children's pictures are not difficult to take at all if we are so familiar with the operation of our camera that we can focus the lens and press the button as quick as lightning. Here, too, the rule is: close in as much as possible and do not stint in film.

The subjects change according to the age of the child. With a baby we are already delighted when we capture a smile, but small children offer innumerable variations of their facial expressions. We must pay particular attention to the most favourable angle of view. The nose appears less pleasing from below, and if we photograph small children standing up their heads will become big and their legs short. Here, too, glaring sunlight is not recommended, but bright light is very acceptable, because it enables us to use high shutter speeds and in addition to stop down a little.

In order to be always ready for action in the close-up range and with upright exposures I do not always refocus for the minor changes in the subject distance caused by head- or to-and-fro movements; I try to stick to the distance I have focused on and simply join in the movement or walk backwards

Top: Girl's head. Deliberate unsharpness in the foreground through the use of a long-focal-length lens. Bottom: From "Porgy and Bess". 135 mm Hektor. Both photographs by Horst H. Baumann.

168

Left:

Quite by accident I came across this Tyrolean peasant family sitting on their doorstep as for a group photograph. My companion's conversation made them relaxed, so that they hardly noticed my photographic intentions. 90 mm Elmarit f/8, ¹/₁₂₅ sec.

Photograph by Kisselbach

Right:

Children's series are particularly rewarding. They will be most natural and successful near the window, with slight softening of the lighting by reflection from a wall or a white sheet. 90 mm Elmar.

Photograph by Nikolai Bogner

and forwards with my model. After a little practice we shall soon know how large the child should appear in the viewfinder, so that he will be sharp in the picture at the distance focused.

We should never "arrange" children when "taking photographs" of them. At home, too, they should be taken "in action". During play, painting, or helping mummy a little with the housework. Naturally, flash is a great help in many a situation, but where the room is small, point the flash at the ceiling to soften the light. (With bounce flash — halve the guide number — proceed by trial and error).

Children should be photographed as they really are, not like little dolls. During the winter, many pictures in the home can be taken on ultra-fast black-and-white film and with 200 W bulbs in the ceiling lamps. Since we can see the effect of the light, we also can judge it better. Small desk lamps or candles can perhaps be included in the picture to attractive effect.

Colour pictures of children are as simple to take as black-and-white ones: The following points should be specially noted:
1) Mixtures of halfwatt light and daylight create great difficulties. Flash and daylight harmonize.
2) Avoid glaring light, i.e. illuminate indirectly, to make sure that the facial expression remains natural.
3) Approach your subject as closely as you can — fill the film format — close-ups, although slightly more difficult, are more effective.
4) Be careful to choose clothing that matches well.

Animals

Specialists in animal photography will soon get to know all the difficulties of the craft; poodle portraiture is comparatively simple; telephoto shots of wild animals in their natural haunts are another matter. Camera safaris in Africa are really rewarding only after we have established a close relationship with our camera. The subjects extend from the tiny insect to the giant pachyderm, involve the whole range of photography.

This pair of Oran Utans was "snapped" with a 35 mm wide-angle lens on the spur of the moment. The photographer held the lens against the fence without looking through the viewfinder. f/8, $^1/_{250}$ sec. Photograph by Kisselbach.

If you want to practise, visit a zoo with free-ranging enclosures. In most zoos photography is permitted, in some you may have to pay a small fee. But because of the need for moats, ditches, etc. the distances to the animals are so great that for results to be satisfactory telephoto lenses are essential. With some animals it is necessary to observe the feeding times. It is worth making enquiries as we enter the zoo and arranging our schedule accordingly. Close-ups of baby animals are most appealing. The more closely we approach, the more precise and reliable must our camera technique be. But animal portraits are worth all the trouble we take over them. Thin wire mesh disappears if it is as close as possible to the camera lens, and the pictures are taken at full aperture; but this requires very accurate focusing. Watch out in front of monkey cages. When the camera is within reach, the inmates are apt to develop an unhealthy interest in it (unhealthy for the camera).

A special field of close-up photography covers the various species of insects. For a number of reasons, here, too, we need medium- to long-focal-length lenses. With short focal lengths the distances between the front lens and the object become very short and make lighting arrangements rather difficult. For a given reproduction scale the longer focal length is also slightly more favourable regarding the depth of field at small apertures. Detailed knowledge of the insects' habits is as important as a suitable photographic outfit. Many insects are less lively in cool weather. Now is the time to photograph them. Under an overcast sky we use flash as a substitute for the sun.

For birds in the nest, too, supplementary flash is very popular. A number of techniques can be used for the shutter release: release by pneumatic tube, electric remote control, or infra-red light trap, which is actuated by the bird itself as it approaches its nest. The last method requires much imagination in order to set the light trap so that the positions photographed are favourable. We must always avoid interference with the animals' habits.

Animal photography ranges over a great many special fields, and the experts are producing results that are truly astonishing. Besides really profound zoological knowledge patience and perseverance are the most essential requirements here. Especially when we stalk big game with the camera the difficulties are very great, because here very long focal lengths become necessary.

If we want to photograph animals at a distance it will often be useful to consider the laws of image formation first. An animal 40 m (132 ft) away, for instance, will appear at $1/800$ its size on a 35 mm film through a 50 mm lens. If it measures 2 m (6 ft 8 in), it will be 2000 mm : 800 = 2.5 mm (80 in : 800 = 0.1 in) on the film.

Aquarium pictures are more difficult to take than it would at first appear. Flash is often completely ruled out. Some fishes take such bad fright that they crash into the aquarium wall and hurt themselves dangerously.

Prohibitions to use flash should be strictly observed especially with large aquarium displays because we might be held responsible for any damage we cause. Photoflood lamps, too, have their drawbacks. In small tanks they quickly raise the temperature of the water by a few degrees. If we leave the cover plates on top of the tanks there is a danger that they burst.

Frontal illumination causes disturbing reflections. Whether we set up our lights at the top, laterally at an angle of 45°, or, if flash is permissible, the flash directly outside the front panel entirely depends on local conditions. The front panel should be clean both outside and inside. For these reasons we can take good colour photographs only when we are quite familiar with the local situation and have made suitable preparations. When we use ultrafast black-and-white films the situation is much simpler because we can manage with the available light combined with large lens apertures.

Close-up photography

There is no clear boundary at which the close-up range can be said to begin, because the various camera designs permit quite different settings. Generally anything smaller than about 40 × 60 cm (16 × 24 in) is regarded as a close-up subject. With most cameras we need accessories in order to obtain sharp results. Since the film format plays a part in the reduction scale, the 35 mm format is preferred here. This format is the most popular; it also boasts of the largest number of accessories for the close-up range. The numerical relations for this format have been used in the description below.

Between the reproduction scales of 1 : 1 and about 25 : 1 we do not speak of close-up photography, but of macrophotography. Still higher magnifications are better obtained with the microscope.

Two different methods are available for the sharp rendering of close-up subjects: 1) Supplementary front lenses, 2) increase of the camera extension by means of intermediate pieces such as fixed extension rings, helical focusing mounts, or devices with variable bellows.

Supplementary front lenses are screwed into or slipped onto the camera lens like filters.

They are preferably used in the close-up range when the normal focusing range is no longer enough. Their refractive power is stated in dioptres as for spectacles. For the close-up range we need collecting lenses; if necessary we can combine 2 such lenses. Their combined refractive power is the two dioptres added together. We can also convert the dioptres into focal lengths: 100 : dioptre = focal length. A supplementary front lens of + 2 dioptres has a focal length of 50 cm.

It is useful to know the focal length because this is the distance (object-supplementary front lens) at which we obtain a sharp image with the camera lens, set at infinity, in connection with the supplementary front lens. The additional helical focusing mount of the camera lens allows us an even closer approach. Accurate focusing presents no problem with the single-lens-reflex camera. For the twin-lens version we require two such front lenses. In addition the parallax between the viewfinder lens and the taking lens must be allowed for.

Supplementary front lenses require no extension factor. In order to obtain a satisfactory picture quality we must stop down to at least f/8. Within the close-up range this is a standard stop if only for reasons of depth of field. If filters and supplementary front lenses are combined, the order should be: camera lens, supplementary front lens, filter.

With viewfinder cameras only the combination suggested by the camera manufacturer should be used so long as our experience in this field is still limited.

Increase of the camera extension. Cameras with interchangeable lenses can have their extension increased by means of adapters and focusing bellows. This principle has been found extremely reliable in practice, because in most conditions the focusing range from infinity to the macro region can be covered continuously.

It is desirable with all close-up subjects that we should be able to see and

Goat's Beard. Such close-ups are most successful from a tripod, which enables us to stop down sufficiently to record all the delicate detail. f/16, ¹/₅₀ sec. Photograph by Josef Perneger.

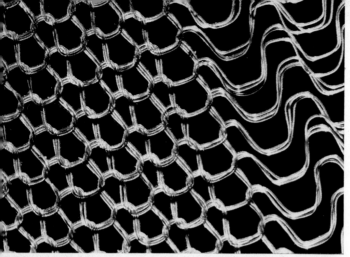

Macrophotograph of a nylon stocking (magnification about 6 times on the negative).
The stocking was held taut across a ring by means of a little elastic band and lit obliquely from below with a projector. f/8, 2 sec.

For aquarium pictures you must distinguish between fishes that are sensitive to flash and those that are sensitive to heat. If you switch on a 500 W lamp vertically above the aquarium for a short period, you can easily take your pictures with a hand-held single-lens-reflex camera. Switch the lamp off soon to avoid heating the water.

This reliquary received supplementary glancing light from a projector, in order to reveal the filigree work of the surface clearly.

We distinguish between line- and halftone reproductions. The most suitable film for both is document-copying film.

This copy of a poem by Christian Morgenstern, a German poet who lived at the beginning of this century, was developed in Rodinal 1:50 for 14 minutes, whereas the copy of the drawing was developed for only 7 minutes. The loss of speed owing to the shorter development is 60 % (4 DIN).

Die zwei Turmuhren

Zwei Kirchturmuhren schlagen hintereinander,
weil sie sonst widereinander schlagen müßten.
Sie vertragen sich wie zwei wahre Christen.
Es wäre dementsprechend zu fragen:
warum nicht auch die Völker
hintereinander statt widereinander schlagen.
Sie könnten doch wirklich ihren Zorn
auslassen, das eine hinten, das andre vorn.
Aber freilich, kleine Beispiele von Vernunft
änderten noch nie etwas am großen Narreteispiel
der Zünft.

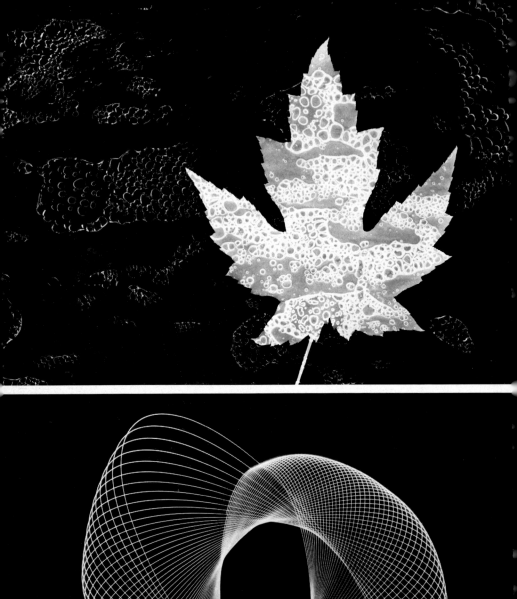
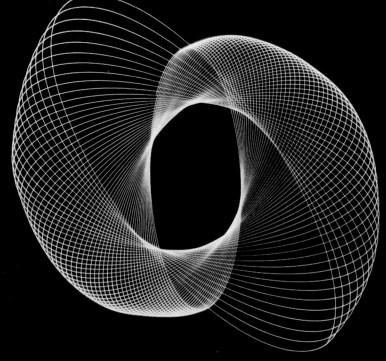

adjust the picture on the focusing screen. This makes reflex cameras ideal. Some measuring-viewfinder system cameras therefore have attachable mirror reflex devices, which are also eminently suitable.

In close-up photography the depth of field is shallow. Here we must consider a law: The depth of field does not depend on the focal length of a lens, but on the reproduction scale. This is the ratio of the original to its image on the film. If we photograph an object measuring 72×108 mm (3×4 in) on a 35 mm film measuring 24×36 mm the object will be reduced to one third of its original size. The reproduction scale is $1 : 3$ or, expressed in decimals, 0.333. The increase in extension necessary to obtain a sharp picture is one third of the focal length of the lens used. For $1 : 2$ we need $1/2$ the focal length, for $1 : 1$ the whole focal length.

The question is often asked what focal length is favourable for close-up photography; it cannot be answered in a single sentence. When the subject is stationary and without depth we can, in theory, work with any focal length. The only limitation of short focal lengths is that the distance between the front member of the camera lens and the subject is very short. This creates difficulties with the lighting arrangements. In practice a longer focal length is therefore preferable; the longer object distance is more convenient, and more space is available for adjusting the lamps. This is important especially in close-up photography of living objects (insects etc.). One limitation is imposed by the fact that a much longer extension will become necessary. At 35 mm focal length and a reproduction scale of $4 : 1$ the additional extension is 140 mm, but 540 mm at 135 mm focal length. We shall often have to fall back on the more intense, but very short electronic flash as our light source.

Any increase in extension above a certain value will require an increase in exposure. The engraved stop numbers are therefore correct only in their ratios, no longer absolutely. The calculation is comparatively simple with ordinary types of lens.

We add the extension increase to the focal length, and square the value obtained, because the diaphragm aperture is an area.

Our example: $(1 + 0.333)^2 = 1.333^2 \approx 1.8$.

Top: Photogram by Hans Steinhorst.
Bottom: Photograph of a swinging pendulum by W. Richter (pp. 184/185).

This extension factor increases enormously once we have entered the range of macrophotography. If we take a picture at 3 × magnification (3 : 1), the calculation will be $(1 + 3)^2 = 4^2 = 16$.

If the exposure is measured through the lens (in modern single-lens-reflex cameras) this calculation becomes unnecessary, because the exposure meter automatically allows for the extension factors. But the focusing light must be very strong to be powerful enough to produce a reading. In certain conditions the light cone of our projector is suitable for this purpose. But we must take care to cut down the contrast of the strongly one-sided light sufficiently by means of a reflecting screen to preserve the modelling without excessive shadows.

If we use telephoto lenses for close-up objects we must bear the following points in mind: The design of these lenses is such as to give them a shorter structural length. The position of the diaphragm differs radically from that in conventional types of lens. If we use these lenses in the near-focusing range the aperture relationship will no longer apply; this increases the extension factor for the exposure considerably. The increase depends on the make of lens, as its types differ. The extension factor is the longer the shorter the structural length of the lens.

Copying

There are two basically different types of original in copying: the *halftone originals*, which must be reproduced as faithfully as possible, and *line originals*, whose rendering may be more contrasty.

If letterpress and halftone subjects are to be copied together, the halftone method must be adopted. Normally we use a tripod or a special copying stand. For parallel lines it is essential that the camera lens is perpendicularly above the point of intersection of the diagonals of the original to be copied. Another condition is perfectly even illumination. For artificial light we use two identical lamps, one on each side of the original. The lamp distance should be long enough to permit a lighting angle no steeper than 45 ° to avoid reflections owing to the sheen of the printing ink. The correct and identical lamp distances are checked by means of a pencil stood on the original directly below the camera lens. Both shadows it casts must be of equal depth.

In daylight we copy at a distance of at least 1 m (40 in) from the window.

The falling-off of the light on the side away from the window is compensated by means of a piece of white cardboard set up so that it reflects the light from the window. For the determination of the exposure time we take our reading off a white area instead of the original itself. We double the value found for line reproductions, and quadruple it for halftone subjects. f/11 is reccommended for all types of copying.

Dark, shiny originals, such as oil paintings and pictures under glass, are among the most difficult subjects for copying. Here, reflections can occur if the camera, too, is illuminated. Small objects are photographed through the hole in a piece of dark cardboard, which must be a little larger than the original. For halftone subjects we use slow, conventional black-and-white film, and give it generous exposure, but cut down on development to compensate for it. We measure the exposure for its rated speed, but, if possible, make a second exposure twice as long.

The so-called document-copying films are of special importance. They have a very high resolving power and inherently a steep gradation. But with suitable methods of development (Rodinal 1 : 50, 7 min. at 20°C) we can also photograph halftone originals with them if a slight increase in contrast is useful. But the exposure latitude of these films is narrow, and it is urgently recommended first to obtain a trial strip at graded exposure times until we are familiar with the material. A suitable extension factor is 1.4, i.e. every other negative is exposed twice as long (e.g. 0.7 — 1 — 1.4 — 2 — 2.8 if the measurement was 1 sec). Depending on the type of development, the speed of these films is 10–13 DIN (8–16 ASA).

When we copy originals in colour we must decide whether we want to use daylight- or artificial-light colour film. Usually a daylight colour film will be in our camera, when direct sunlight or diffuse daylight will be suitable. We do not place the original on the ground, but fix it upright (on a wall etc.); this reduces the risk of reflection. Again we must ensure angle-true alignment (lens pointing at the centre of the original). Precise determination of the exposure time is important and the extension factor must be allowed for with small originals. If we use electronic flash, we can use it similarly indoors. The flash holder must not be mounted on the camera, but set up to the left or the right of it. On the side opposite the flash we soften the shadows with a piece of white cardboard, unless we can use two flash holders.

Special exposure techniques

By this we obviously do not mean the accidental double exposure, but the intentional addition of pictorial impressions as effective elements of composition. The procedure is comparatively simple if we have a camera whose shutter can be released repeatedly without film transport. The majority of modern cameras, however, have been designed with a special lock that prevents us from taking a second exposure on the same piece of film. The tricks we have to use to obtain our double exposure vary from model to model and can therefore not be explained here.

Mirror-reflex cameras are especially suitable for this purpose; here we can enter special auxiliary markings on the focusing screen so that we know precisely the limits of the picture area for the 2nd and 3rd or more exposures. Usually a fairly dark background is essential so that after the exposure of the first picture some unexposed space is left for the further exposures.

At first we play

We play chess against ourselves, advance from there to portrait studies, combine a shadow profile with a frontal aspect. Today advertising photography has become interested in multiple exposures, because they lend themselves to skilfully combining representations of operating instructions, outer wrapping, and internal function into an effective picture.

Photograms

are part of "exposure technique without a camera". To all practical purposes a photogram is a shadow picture. More or less opaque subjects are placed on light-sensitive paper. The subsequent exposure to white light changes the emulsion so that all the portions fully affected by the light will become black in the subsequent development process. Partly opaque objects produce grey values. Especially for the beginner the setting up of photograms is good practice to become familiar with the photographic grey values. We use enlarging paper no smaller than 18×24 cm (10×8 in).

For the set-up we can use the ordinary yellow-green darkroom safelight for the positive process. For the exposure a simple halfwatt-lamp (ceiling light) is suitable. Sometimes the light cone of our enlarger, without negative of course, can also be used. We first determine the exposure with the aid of a small trial strip. This is particularly important if not only black and white, but also grey tones are to be reproduced. When developing the trial strips we must adhere to the prescribed developing time.

Light pendulum

The light pendulum is one of the most attractive experiments, which can be carried out with even the simplest equipment. Owing to the effect of gravity the path of the pendulum changes with every movement. To record the movement with the camera we need a small pocket torch, which we suspend from the ceiling on a length of stout thread so that its height above the floor is about 1.5 m (5 ft), and a dark room; so that only a point of light is produced we have to use a bulb with an almost point-shaped filament, and remove the condenser lens in front of it. At the back we mask the bulb by pushing it through a hole of about 50 mm diameter in a piece of black cardboard. Suspension of the pocket torch is comparatively simple. We just drill a little hole in the centre of the screw cap for the battery, lead the thread through and secure it with one or two knots.

We place the camera, lens facing upwards, on the floor beneath the pocket torch. When the pendulum, with the pocket torch switched on, is made to swing, the curve it describes will be recorded on the film if we keep the shutter permanently open by means of a cable release. The lens stop depends on the film speed (with medium-speed film f/8); the lens is focused on 1.5 m (5 ft). Exposure time: 20 sec to 1 min.

At 1.5 m (5 ft) focusing distance a 50 mm lens covers a field measuring about 60 × 90 cm (24 × 36 in), a 35 mm wide-angle lens one of about 100 × 150 cm (40 × 60 in) for the pendulum to swing in.

We can change the figures of the pendulum swing very widely if we tie the thread, not to a single point on the ceiling, but to another thread which in turn is fixed to two points.

Colour pictures of pendulum swings, too, are very interesting. We can place colour filters or foils on the camera lens during the exposure, and thus differentiate the record on the film. Disturbing flare is prevented by the very effective antihalation protection of the colour reversal film.

185

DARKROOM TECHNIQUE

Developing his own films and printing his own enlargements has for many years been a characteristic of the serious amateur. The growing popularity of colour photography has reduced the number of darkroom addicts. Various causes, such as the mechanization of the photofinisher's darkroom and the fiveday week have revived the wish of many to work in a darkroom of their own.

The advantage of this is not so much financial; it is the pleasure of creating something, of achieving something guided by our own imagination. In our day and age, when so many activities are split up by organization, it is a source of satisfaction to be able to carry an operation through from beginning to end.

Negative development

After the exposure the image is not yet visible on the film, it is "latent". A special process, development, reduces the exposed silver halide crystals to metallic silver. The developer is oxidized during this reaction. In addition to the special developing agent it contains a preservative to protect it from too rapid oxidation. To accelerate the developing process, the solution is made alkaline. In order to confine development to the exposed crystals only, potassium bromide or some other anti-foggant is added to the developer. Both time and temperature have an influence on development; so has agitation and the number of films already developed in the solution.

It is best to buy the developer ready-packed. Instructions make it easy to prepare the correct solution or dilution. Developing our own films has a number of advantages and above all offers the possibility of influencing the result. Machine development, which has now been generally adopted by the photofinishers, is quite acceptable for average results, but in view of the large throughput of films it is practically impossible to consider individual wishes. We save nothing by developing our own films, but we can learn very much about refined photographic techniques by doing so.

All we need besides the few appliances and a completely darkened room is sufficient accuracy to adhere to the correct times and the correct temperatures. Here is a detailed account of darkroom practice:

Our working gear consists of a developing tank, a measure, a thermometer and a watch. A darkroom safelight is not essential, we can insert the film in the tank in complete darkness; but it does make it easier to find one's way about. The eye requires about 8–10 minutes until it is used to the dark-green light.

There are two types of developing tanks: plastic ones and those made of stainless steel. Plastic tanks are cheaper, but breakable, steel is practically indestructible. Since threading the film requires a certain amount of dexterity with all tanks, we should practise this with a piece of old film in daylight — until we can do it with our eyes closed. Some tanks are a little on the small side; here we must trim the lead off 35 mm films before loading them on the spiral.

The developing device consists of the spiral, the tank, and the lid, which closes it light-tight. This allows the development to be carried out in daylight. The prescribed volume of developer is poured into the tank. The normal temperature is 20 °C. The ordinary spirit thermometers react very slowly, taking almost a minute to give the correct reading. Shortly after it is filled, the tank is tapped on the table several times in order to dislodge any air bubbles from the film. During the developing process the developer must be mixed thoroughly. Simple rotation of the spiral is not sufficient for this purpose. Tanks that can be turned upside-down (inversion tanks) have been found very useful; we divide the whole developing time into 10 intervals, inverting the tank once per interval.

During the developing process, potassium bromide is liberated from generously exposed areas, where it inhibits the developing process, causing schlieren unless it is evenly distributed in the developer solution by means of this agitation. Developing times under 5 minutes are impractical in tanks, because part of the time of pouring out and of intermediate rinse must be included in them. Here it will be preferable to dilute the developer further.

The developing time itself depends on the properties of the film and of the developer used. With normal development the completely exposed film lead should be blackened only enough for a light source to be dimly visible through it after fixing. The advantage of normal development consists in the possibility of balancing the various contrasts, and even very different subjects can be readily printed or enlarged.

The developing time recommended by the maker can mostly be cut down by 1–2 minutes. The loss of film speed will still be very slight, but the compensation of contrasty subjects will be considerably better. The number of films that can be developed in a 1000 cc solution depends on various factors. In the directions enclosed with the product we shall find indications of the developing time for more than 2 films. Some types of developer, however, can be used only once (Rodinal, Neofin) and must be freshly made up for every film. It is advisable to stick to a well-tried formula, whose properties will soon be familiar.

Pouring the solution away takes about 20 seconds, and must be fully added to the developing time; if we give the recommended intermediate rinse, 10–15 seconds of this must also be added to it. But if we work with a stop bath (see formula p. 201), the developing process is at once stopped, and no time should be allowed for here.

After the tank has been emptied, fixing solution (see formula p. 201) of about the same temperature as that of the developer is poured into the tank. Duration of fixing 5–10 min, shorter for ultra-fine-grain, longer for faster films. The fixing solution can be used repeatedly, for up to 12 35 mm or rollfilms per 1000 cc. It is not advisable to use the same fixing bath for both films and photographic papers.

In the fixing solution the unexposed silver bromide is dissolved without the blackened silver being attacked to any great extent. The reaction itself is very complicated. The film should therefore be fixed for twice the time it takes to clear it completely. The times recommended for this process are ample.

After the fixing bath has been returned to its bottle the film must be rinsed so that the residual chemicals are washed out, because only then will the film acquire good storage properties. The final rinse, too, must be carried out in the tank because the risk of scratching the very sensitive gelatine layer is otherwise far too great. Rinsing time: 20 minutes in slowly running water, or 6 changes of water, one every five minutes, where running water is not available. The water is not used for rinsing, only for a slow diffusing-out of the residual salts.

In order to avoid the occurrence of drying marks, we bathe the film briefly in a wetting agent (formula p. 201), and hang it up to dry in a dust-free room from a peg at the top, and weighted with another one at the bottom.

The gradation of the negative can be influenced both by the choice of the exposure material (film) and by the developing time. Shorter development produces a softer, conversely, longer development produces a harder gradation. To a certain extent the choice of paper reestablishes the balance where necessary.

Top: Soft gradation

Middle: Normal gradation

Bottom: Vigorous gradation

Medium contrast is recommended in the interest of simplifying darkroom work.

These step wedges are made by means of a Scheiner densitometer. The exposure is graduated with a rotating disc with a stepped circumference.

Soft   *Normal*   *Hard*

To demonstrate the differences between the gradations clearly, prints were made of this negative on paper grades Soft to Hard. Correct assessment of the negative contrast is part of an efficient darkroom routine.

To begin with it is urgently recommended to make trial strips as shown on p. 192 of a soft, of a normal, and of a hard negative.

Top: negative
2nd from top: soft
3rd from top: normal
Bottom: hard

1

1,4

2

2,8

4

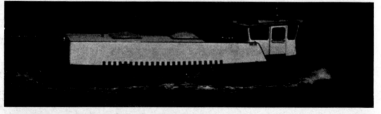

5,6

The film dries much more quickly if we wipe the surplus water off. Various methods can be used, and several aids are available for this process. It involves a small risk. The film must be securely clamped at the top if we wipe it down with a pair of wet rubber tongs. If we are nimble, we can wipe the film between index- and middle finger, but must be sure to take our rings off (if any). Moist absorbent cotton wool or a moist piece of chamois leather (must be absolutely dust-free) are also suitable for this purpose.

If we speed up drying with a fan, we increase the risk of dust settling on the emulsion. The modern thin-emulsion films dry normally within a few hours. It is not advisable to keep the films wound up in rolls; keeping them in translucent negative sleeves is preferable; 35 mm films in strips of 6, 6 × 6 ($2^{1}/_{4}$ × $2^{1}/_{4}$ in) films in strips of 3. Any tendency of 35 mm films to curl inwards must be countered by means of winding them emulsion side outwards and keeping them like this for 5–6 hours.

DEVELOPERS

For medium and ultra-fast films the modern finegrain developers are recommended. They do not produce excessive contrast, in spite of good film speed utilization. Examples are Atomal (Agfa-Gevaert), Microdol (Kodak), Microphen (Ciba-Ilford), Promicrol (May & Baker), Ultrafin (Tetenal) etc. The manufacturer's instructions contain detailed information about developing times of the various films.

Rodinal (Agfa-Gevaert) is a special developer for influencing the gradation of slow, contrasty films and document-copying films towards "normal" and "soft". A dilution of 1:50 has been found very reliable; developing time 5–14 minutes depending on the film and the desired gradation. The diluted developer is used only once and then discarded. It is not a finegrain developer, so that it should be used only for films with inherently fine grain. Its resolving power and definition are excellent.

The exposure series opposite was taken with the factor 1.4, which always doubles the next but one exposure. The beginner is recommended to make exposure trials of the same picture area on several paper grades at several exposure times, and to develop, fix, rinse, and dry the prints normally. Absolutely correct assessment of the picture is possible only in the dry state.

Tips for developing

> The temperature of the developer should be exactly 20 °C. If the work-room is colder or warmer we place the developing tank in a large bowl filled with water at 20 °C. This water bath keeps the temperature constant for a long time.

> The amateur will find it uneconomical to make up his own developer from the various constituents. Buying the chemicals in small quantities increases their price, if we buy them in larger quantities we run the risk of some substances deteriorating through age and endangering results.

> The developer solution should be free from suspended particles; this is achieved by filtering. Fairly coarse filter paper inserted in a funnel is adequate for our purpose. Timers with bell signals are very practical for film development; we can work in complete darkness.

> The developing time recommended by the manufacturer is only a guide. The different lime content (hardness) of the water supply affects some developers. Check the density of the completely blackened film lead.

> After the film has been threaded into the spiral of the tank we cut the end torn from the cassette spool off to avoid possible damage when the still wet film curls inwards after removal from the spiral.

> Increased developing time, it is true, improves film speed utilization; but it also increases contrast and graininess. Very short developing times (less than 5 minutes) are not recommended. There is a risk of schlieren formation. Likewise, development without agitation may produce uneven patches, bands, and other faults. Very strong agitation leads to over-development along the edges or picture margins.

> Atmospheric oxygen weakens the power of the developer. We therefore must fill the bottles completely. Soft polythene bottles are very useful for this purpose. When they are only half full, we squeeze them before screw-ing the top on so that only little air remains above the developer solution.

> All bottles should have a label indicating contents and date of making up.

> Developer solutions should be stored in brown bottles or in darkness.

194

Tips for fixing

> In the fixing solution, too, we must agitate the film at first.

> If we are in a hurry we use rapid fixing salt. It cuts down the fixing time to 2–4 minutes. The final rinse, too, is a little shorter than after an ordinary fixing bath.

> Splashes of hypo in the darkroom must be avoided. Hypo dust causes spots on undeveloped film.

> If we occasionally have to develop several films at a time, we save a lot of time as well as chemicals if we use one tank for development, but do not empty it, carrying out the subsequent processes – intermediate rinse, fixing, and final rinse – in separate tanks or vessels, on the conveyor belt principle as it were.

Enlarging technique

Enlarging is comparatively easy to learn. The yellow-green darkroom light is bright enough for us to see clearly and to control every phase. It is more than ever advisable today to do this at home, because the usual small album prints are copied or enlarged mostly by machines. We can speak of a picture only from the 18 × 24 cm (8 × 10 in) format upwards; only then will picture quality really be revealed. To enable our eyes to adapt themselves completely to the darkroom illumination, we must arrange all the lamps so that we cannot see the light bulbs directly.

THE BASIC PROCESS OF ENLARGING

The enlarger consists of the lamp housing, the negative stage, and the enlarging lens. It can be vertically adjusted for changing the enlarging ratio. The light is collected by a condenser so that the negative is transilluminated as evenly as possible. Unless our enlarger is of the autofocusing type, the lens must be focused on the distance of the enlarging paper.

The negative is held in the negative stage emulsion side downwards. The light-sensitive enlarging paper is inserted in the masking frame on the baseboard. We develop it for 1½–2 minutes in a paper developer after exposure, give it an intermediate rinse, fix it, rinse it thoroughly, and dry it.

Not all of us will be able to set up a darkroom of our own, but we can obtain good results even with a temporary set-up. We protect the table from developer- and hypo stains by covering it with plastic foil.

The room must be blacked out. In the evening this presents few problems, since it need by no means be as lightproof as a negative darkroom. The simplest darkroom safelights are the tinted light bulbs by Osram and Philips. They can be inserted in a desk lamp and set up so that the beam path of the enlarger is in the shade, but the developer and hypo dishes are well lit. We generally keep them at a distance of 60 cm (24 in). The bulb should be screened so that it is not directly visible.

Absolute cleanliness is quite essential. The enlarger and the storage area for the enlarging paper must be protected against splashes. The dishes should be arranged so that spilling of solution is avoided during development. We use print tongs so that we need not dip our hands alternately into the baths. Each bath should have its own clearly marked tongs. Depending on room conditions we can set up the dry and the wet side so that we have to turn through 90° or 180° from one to the other. Before we insert the negative in the negative stage we switch the light of the enlarger on, so that we can inspect the surface of the negative for dust. Tiny pieces of fluff etc. are removed with a sable brush. The negative is now inserted in the negative stage. If ordinary glass plates press against the back of the negative, Newton's rings can be caused by extremely thin air cushions, whose images in interference colours will show up especially in uniform areas. We can avoid them by the use of etched glass pressure plates, which have a very fine surface structure.

We do not focus on the dead centre of the picture, but on the zone between the centre and the margin. Recommended stop: f/8, for the highest demands of sharpness f/11. If the negative has no detail that can easily be focused, it is best to replace it with a negative of letter-press, focus this, and exchange it again for the negative to be enlarged. A 2–3 × magnifier should be used to check the focusing. More powerful ones are unsuitable, because they interfere with the beam path of the enlarger.

The brightness of the enlarger lamp has a certain influence on the brilliance of the enlargement; likewise, spotlessly clean surfaces of the condenser and the enlarging lens produce contrastier results.

Exposure timer. An exposure timer, of which there are various versions, is more accurate and convenient than counting. The use of exposure times below 2 seconds is not recommended if there is printing-up or holding back to be done. For professional purposes automatic exposure timers have been available for some time; they are electronically controlled, and their measurement takes the sensitivity of the bromide paper, negative density, and quantity of light into account.

The bromide paper should be kept where it is well protected from stray light. A pre-exposure below the threshold, although it does not yet fog the paper, alters its gradation towards "soft". With large formats the risk of stray-light exposure exists when the enlarger is set up too close to bright walls.

Pictorial composition in the darkroom through printing up or holding back of certain portions of the negative and choice of the best picture area are some of the most important factors in favour of the amateur producing his own enlargements. There is no need to keep slavishly to the prescribed proportions of the paper format. With large formats we cut off the part that is not going to be used before we expose, so that the paper saved can serve as a trial strip.

Bromide (enlarging) papers are available in various grades. If the negative is contrasty, we compensate for this by using a soft-grade paper. Conversely, we enlarge a soft negative on contrasty paper. Judgement of the negative gradation and the correct choice of paper grade is not very easy for the beginner. Here, too, trial and error is best, and we use several paper grades as trial strips.

Printing exposure series on various paper grades is an excellent exercise for obtaining an idea of the changes in the positive. The trial exposures are made according to a fixed scheme, of the same area, of the same dimensions, and the paper is developed for the same time. The shortest exposure time should be such that a very light picture is produced by normal development. The various grades of paper differ in their sensitivity. With the "Hard" and "Extra hard" grades the exposure factor for the series must be smaller to produce sufficient intermediate steps. After fixing, rinsing, and drying, all exposure steps are classified according to paper grades and mounted on a sheet of cardboard. So that we can sort them out correctly we mark them on the back with a very soft pencil before exposing them. This mounted layout will provide us with very valuable indications for our subsequent trial strips, because we can now calculate the approximately correct exposure time from the print density. The expense of paper and effort will pay for itself several times over, because we shall be able to determine the correct exposure times much more quickly.

Photographic papers are produced not only in various grades, but also with various surfaces. In the beginning, before we have acquired sufficient experience, we should work only with "White glossy". Furthermore, we should strictly adhere to the recommended developing time. Only later, with some experience, should we use papers with different surfaces. All matt surfaces dry darker. When wet they must therefore appear a trifle lighter than the "White glossy" version. In print assessment the distance of the darkroom lamp plays an important part, so that we must ensure constant conditions.

It is essential to keep the developer temperature at 20° C. A stop bath should be introduced after development; the prints should be repeatedly agitated in the fixing bath. Fixing should not exceed 10 minutes; the prints are now immersed in tap water. Even during the rinse of about 20 minutes in running water we must ensure that the prints do not adhere to one another. If no running water is available, the water should be renewed 5 to 6 times at 5-minute intervals. We must bear in mind that the reason for rinsing is not the washing off, but the diffusion of the fixing salts.

The advanced worker will not merely expose his print, he will often either hold back or print up certain parts of the picture. For this purpose he uses "dodges" of various shapes on wire handles, and holes in sheets of dark cardboard respectively, which he moves slightly during the exposure, so that the transition to the neighbouring, unaffected parts of the print is less noticeable. The times of these special exposures can also be determined by trial strips and recorded. As a general rule a ratio of 1 : 2 of main and supplementary exposure times should not be exceeded; otherwise this trick will show up in the print.

There are two methods of positive development: one uses a single developer of medium strength, the other a soft and a contrasty positive developer. We can influence the paper grade also with the developing process and are thus able to adapt the print even better to the character of the negative. Neutol (Agfa-Gevaert) is a developer of the first type. Matched developers for the second method are Centrabrom (soft) and Eukobrom (more vigorous), both by Tetenal.

Negatives of architectural subjects suffer from converging verticals if the film plane of the camera had not been vertical during the exposure. We can correct these lines at the enlarging stage by means of special devices which allow the tilting of both the negative stage and the masking frame according to Scheimpflug's Rule.

If the convergence is only slight, we can compensate it by raising one side of the masking frame and stopping the enlarging lens down to f/11 or f/16. The side of the paper further away from the lens must receive more exposure. After the final rinse the prints are dried either in air or in an electrically heated dryer-glazer. For drying in air we stack the wet prints on top of one another, emulsion side upwards, and squeeze the surplus water out by means of a roller squeegee. We now place them, singly, emulsion side downwards on a linen cloth or on a sheet of white filter paper.

With hot-drying in a dryer-glazer we must make sure that the prints are heat resistant. Almost all glossy papers are. If not, it will say so on the packing paper or box. With other surfaces heat drying is undesirable as it affects them unfavourably, and it is advisable to test a waste strip of paper whether it will stand this treatment. Insufficiently hardened surfaces can be after-hardened in a 4 % formalin solution.

Treatment in a 1 % wetting agent solution produces a better gloss. Glossy papers dry at high gloss if we squeegee them emulsion side down on to a chromium-plated brass sheet. The glazing sheet must be spotlessly clean, and should therefore be rinsed thoroughly under running water before use. The dripping wet prints are placed on it emulsion side down, and the surplus water is removed with a roller-squeegee or in a mangle. The glazing sheet is held down on the dryer-glazer by an apron under tension, which must not be released before the prints are completely dry.

When we remove the prints from the hot press they will, to begin with, curl very strongly; we spread them on a cool support. As soon as they have taken up a little moisture they will lie flat again.

Spotting — trimming

A print is not finished until it has been spotted and trimmed. The method of spotting depends on whether the paper is matt or glossy. Matt papers can be spotted in the light and medium tones with retouching pencils (Negro or Zulu). For the dark shadows a brush is better.

For the spotting of glossy prints we need two good sable brushes, a tube of positive retouching dye, neutral black glossy. A little dye is transferred to a porcelain plate. The brush is first dipped in water and drawn across filter paper so that it contains just the right amount of moisture. We now take up enough retouching dye from the porcelain plate to obtain no more than a light-grey stroke with the brush. We now practise on waste prints so that we transfer only enough dye to make the tiny light spots and wriggles disappear. For glossy prints we can mix the retouching dye with a little gum arabic to make it a little glossier.

Black spots and lines must be removed by knifing; this is successful only with a perfectly honed scraping knife. We move it very gently across the offending spot — until the tone of the spot approximately matches that of the surrounding area. If we have scraped off too much we must build the tone up again with retouching dye. With glossy prints, knifing is the first step. The prints are then soaked and glazed again, and only now spotted.

After-treatment

By means of silver solvents the silver can again be combined with halides both in the negative and in the positive; they can now bee toned, redeveloped, or dissolved (reduction). All these after-treatments involve a certain amount of risk. They are preferably carried out on positives, because the original negative remains unaffected.

Farmer's Reducer is the best-known solution for after-treatment. It increases contrast, clears the highlights, lightens shadows and can also be used partially. It can be applied immediately after fixing, but calls for a thorough rinse afterwards. The solution decomposes very quickly. This must be allowed for when we practise on a waste print.

FORMULAE

Stop bath

for positives

water	1000 cc
glacial acetic acid (98 %)	20 cc
or glacial acetic acid (28 %)	70 cc

for negatives and positives

water	1000 cc
potassium metabisulphite	40 g

Reducers for negatives and positives

FARMER'S REDUCER

Solution A		Solution B	
water	100 cc	water	1000 cc
potassium ferricyanide	10 g	sodium thiosulphate cryst.	100 g

Mixture for working solution:

Solution A   5—10 cc
Solution B   100 cc
Mix immediately before use. Mixture does not keep long.

Fixing solutions

FIXING BATH

water (about 50° C)	750 cc
sodium thiosulphate cryst.	250 cc
potassium metabisulphite	25 g
water to	1000 cc

RAPID FIXING BATH

water (about 50° C)	750 cc
sodium thiosulphate cryst.	250 cc
ammonium chloride	50 g
potassium metabisulphite	25 g
water to	1000 cc

Wetting agent

e.g. Agepon dilution 1 : 200
Immersion for about $1/2$—1 min
With films it is preferable to use distilled water for dilution.

201

INDEX